Legacy of a '60s

Em & Moo

Legacy of a '60s Female Rock Duo

Em & Moo

By Kathy Bushnell

A Memoir

Wisdom House Books

Em & Moo

Legacy of a '60s Female Rock Duo

Published by Wisdom House Books, Inc.
Chapel Hill, North Carolina 27516 USA
1.919.883.4669 | www.wisdomhousebooks.com

Wisdom House Books is committed to excellence in the publishing industry.

Book design copyright © 2020 by Wisdom House Books, Inc. All rights reserved.

Cover and Interior Design by Ted Ruybal

Published in the United States of America

Paperback ISBN: 978-1-7348222-0-5
LCCN: 2020908426

BIO026000 | BIOGRAPHY & AUTOBIOGRAPHY / Personal Memoirs
BIO004000 | BIOGRAPHY & AUTOBIOGRAPHY / Music
BIO022000 | BIOGRAPHY & AUTOBIOGRAPHY / Women

First Edition

25 24 23 22 21 20 / 10 9 8 7 6 5 4 3 2 1

All of the events, locales, and conversations in this memoir are true to the best of the
author's memory. The views expressed in this memoir are solely those of the author.
The reader should not consider this book anything other than a work of literature.

Dedication

For Janet, Jesse, and Regina.

"Do You Believe in Magic?"

—John Sebastian—
The Lovin' Spoonful

"I'm Going to Change the World"

—Eric Burdon—
The Animals

Table of Contents

Prologue

Colston Hall 1969

Em and I were waiting in the wings at Colston Hall in Bristol, UK. Our female rock duo was about to open a concert for the popular rock band Family, and I was nervously shifting from one foot to the other. The house was packed with a capacity crowd of more than two thousand fans. Out on the stage, our Telecaster electric guitars were plugged into the megalithic stacks of Marshall amplifiers. Two microphones in their stands had been set up for us by the roadies. My Hohner blues harmonicas were lined up in a row on top of one of the amplifiers, where I had placed them earlier.

I watched as our manager, Tony Gourvish, walked to the center of the stage and leaned in towards one of the microphones.

"All the way from America (dramatic pause) . . . Please give a special welcome to EMILY MUFF!"

The audience began to applaud as he disappeared into the wings.

My bandmate and I rushed onstage, blinking in the glare of the spotlights overhead. Em slung the strap of her Telecaster over her shoulder while I grabbed one of my Hohner harmonicas. Then we stepped up to our microphones.

"It's wonderful to be here!" she announced, and then we began to play.

Our chick rock duo performed all Emily Muff original numbers that night, and the final one an instrumental on our two electric guitars. "This last number is called 'Essence,'" Janet informed the audience. I poised my pick over the fretboard of my guitar and began to play the opening bars. Soon, my bandmate had joined in with me. Our notes were melodic yet powerful as they soared throughout the venue.

The crowd leaned forward in their seats, watching . . . curious . . . listening . . .

When the final notes of "Essence" faded away, Colston Hall was filled with thunderous applause. Over two thousand fans were rising from their seats to give our rock duo a standing ovation!

Em and I bowed to the audience. Their cheers followed us as we made our way back to the wings. I nearly bumped into Roger Chapman, vocalist for the band Family, who had been watching our performance.

He smiled, slapped the two of us on our backs, and said, "You chicks are going to be a hard act to follow!"

Chapter One

Rolling Stones Versus Beatles

The tiny transistor radio lying nearby on my bed crackled with static as I tackled my algebra homework on a blustery night in November of 1965. Gusts of wintery wind swirling through the fire escape outside my family's New York City apartment were rattling my window pane. I hadn't been paying much attention to what DJ Murray the K was saying . . . until I heard him announce the rumor that members of the Rolling Stones might be stopping by for drinks later that night at the Phone Booth Club in midtown Manhattan. By that time, the DJ had my *full* attention, and I hastily scribbled the name "Phone Booth" next to a quadratic equation. My math textbook tumbled to the floor as I reached over and turned up the volume on the radio.

When the popular New York City disc jockey repeated the rumor again several minutes later, the homework assignment had been totally abandoned, and my mind was racing at breakneck speed.

WOW!

The Rolling Stones in midtown Manhattan!

REALLY?

"We'll be right back after a word from our sponsor . . ." Murray the K was saying.

"And I'll be right back after a word with Mick and Keith!" I muttered with a grin. I knew I had to get my 16-year-old ass to that club, somehow. But first, I had to find out where this Phone Booth Club was located, and whether the rumor was true. So, I switched off the radio and made a beeline for the telephone book in my father's study. En route, it felt as though drummer Keith Moon was hammering away on a Ludwig in my chest. "Ohh! I can't believe I might meet the Rolling Stones tonight!" I shrieked. My fingers were trembling as I grabbed a copy of the Yellow Pages and began flipping through the book. Once I found the number for the club, I used my family's rotary dial telephone to make the call, and (impatiently!) waited for someone to answer.

"Good evening! Phone Booth!" a guy at the other end of the line announced.

"Umm . . . yes . . ." I began. "Can you tell me if the Rolling Stones have made a reservation at your club tonight?" The Phone Booth employee hesitated for a moment, and then informed me that members of the Rolling Stones had not yet made an appearance, but were expected to arrive shortly.

"Would you like to make a reservation?" he asked.

"No thank you," I fibbed, and promptly hung up the receiver. The truth was that I longed to have booked a table at this mid-Manhattan venue. However, I knew that my parents might have some reservations of their own when it came to allowing their daughter to meet these famous rock 'n' roll rebels. As I exited my father's study, I resisted the urge to grab my coat and head for the door. After all, it was freezing outside, past 10:00 PM, and I had very little cash stashed away in a shoebox under my bed. The only set of "wheels" I owned was a pair of rusty roller skates stored in my bedroom closet. Most of all, however, I was just too chicken to sneak out behind my parents' backs and venture out solo to some unknown club in the dark of night.

It was obvious that my only hope of getting there was to convince my older brother Alan, who was a staunch Beatles fan, that he wanted to go with me. With this in mind, I should have rushed around the apartment in search of my sibling. However, the adolescent urge to check out the gear in my bedroom closet was so overwhelming that I veered off in that direction, instead. Soon, I was rifling through my wardrobe and tossing the various rejects onto the bed. As the pile grew higher, it was clear that I had no special Meet-the-Rolling-Stones outfits from which to choose. "Ugh! There's absolutely *nothing* to wear around here!" I groaned.

I changed out of the casual clothes I'd been wearing, and slipped on some silver, glitter pantyhose. Next, I grabbed a burgundy minidress from the top of the clothing heap. After tugging it over my head, I arranged my long blonde hair into a copy-cat version of British model Pattie Boyd's stylish coif. Then I tugged on a pair of knee-high black leather boots. I was checking out my image in the mirror a final time, when I heard a knock on my bedroom door. Alan entered the room and pointed to the mound of clothing on my bed.

"Holy shit! Are you planning to sleep on that mess tonight?" he asked.

"Actually, I'm planning to meet the Rolling Stones, instead!"

"Oh, yeah . . . sure," my sibling replied in a sarcastic tone of voice. I placed my hands on my hips and explained that DJ Murray the K had just announced that the Stones were supposed to show up that night at a place called the Phone Booth Club in Manhattan. Alan shook his head. "How do you know the rumor's not a bunch of PHONE-Y bologna?" he retorted. I rolled my eyes at his obnoxious pun, and huffed.

"Because I just called the club, and was told that the Stones are gonna be there!" Upon hearing this, my brother seemed to back off a bit, and I took the opportunity to ask whether he would accompany me to the venue.

"What? No way!" he hissed. "It's fucking freezing outside! Why should I waste my time? Besides . . . the Beatles are clearly a superior band." Before we knew it, the two of us had slipped into one of our familiar Beatles versus Stones shouting matches. Although I loved the Mop-Tops, too, I couldn't resist egging my brother on.

"Millions of people think the Rolling Stones are great, and they can't all be wrong," I challenged him. My sibling shook his head, and shot me a scathing glance. Alan was a senior at New York City's High School of Music and Art; it was difficult to argue with him about many things, especially music theory.

"That's a load of bull!" he countered. "Everyone knows that the Beatles have great harmonies, groovy melodies, and meaningful lyrics . . ."

"OK! OK! I agree that they have terrific harmonies." As our altercation continued to escalate, my brother raised his arms in exasperation and started heading towards the door. I raced after him, my voice echoing down the hallway as I begged him to take me to the club. When I finally caught up with Alan in the kitchen, he was leaning nonchalantly against the fridge. As he brushed his long brown hair away from his eyes, the grin on his face was so smug and self-assured, it seemed to rearrange his facial features. "I hope you realize that if I agree to take you to the club, it means you owe me one," he announced.

"Oh, no!" I gulped. "Like . . . what exactly do you have in mind?"

"Well, for starters, you can clean up my room for the next six months . . ."

"What? Ugh! Even meeting Keith Richards isn't worth tackling that grossed-out mess," I bluffed.

"Well, tough luck, then!" my brother snapped. He opened the fridge and popped open a can of soda, while I decided to try a different angle. I smiled sweetly at him, and suggested that I ask our parents to lend me the money for him to take us in a taxi to the Phone Booth Club. Alan was silent for a moment. It seemed as though he was about to relent and he finally nodded his head. I rushed over, gave him a quick hug, and then dashed out of the kitchen towards Mom and Dad's room. As I knocked on their bedroom door, my sibling sauntered up behind me.

"Come on in!" our father called out. I pushed open the door, and the two of us entered the room. Mom and Dad were seated on their king-sized bed. Several stacks of notebooks and various professional journals lay scattered on the chenille spread. I knew that they were busy working on one of their psychological/anthropology articles that were slated for publication. Their deadline was fast-approaching, and I was grateful for the time they took to listen to my request.

"I know it's late, but . . . you know how much I dig the Rolling Stones! Oh, PLEASE let me go to the club!" I implored them. As I spoke, I noticed that a tiny grin had formed at one corner of my father's mouth. He must have been remembering my bedroom, which was plastered wall-to-wall with glossy photos of both the Rolling Stones and the Beatles.

Since the moment our parents had entered into the equation, the bickering between Alan and me had stopped. After much deliberation, they gave the two of us some cash, and their permission to drop by the Phone Booth Club provided that:

1. My brother accompanied me by cab to the venue.

2. The two of us remained together at all times.

3. We left the club by midnight.

4. My sibling escorted me safely back home.

Alan officially agreed to the outing, and I flashed him a grateful smile. Once the remaining details had been finalized, I gave my parents a round of effusive hugs, and then my brother and I headed for the closet in the foyer.

After shrugging on our coats, we rang for the elevator and then exited the apartment building. Soon, the two of us were riding in the Checker cab that my brother had hailed. Its interior was spacious, and we stretched out our legs as the taxi traveled down several side streets before entering Central Park. While we wended our way along the various winding roads, my brother's mood seemed to lighten. At one point, he even confessed that he'd only been joking earlier about my having to clean his room.

Although I was relieved that Alan had rescinded his outrageous demand, I continued to struggle with the double standards that our parents adopted when they set rules regarding the two of us. While I could understand Mom and Dad's concern for my safety, their insistence that my brother escort me to many of the same places they allowed him to go solo was a bitter pill for me to swallow. Luckily, my annoyance with society's double standards had (temporarily) melted away by the time the cab emerged from the park. As the vehicle sped through the East Side of town, I was growing more excited by the minute thinking about the Rolling Stones—and wondering whether my outfit would pass muster with members of this famous band. At the very least, I hoped that I wouldn't faint, freeze-up, or say something ludicrous if I came face-to-face with Mick and Keith.

When the driver finally pulled up outside the Phone Booth Club, my brother paid the fare while I took a moment to glance outside the window. I had fully expected to see a line of Rolling Stones fans snaking around the block, or the entranceway jam-packed with groupies fighting for a chance to gain access to the club.

Instead, the area was eerily empty.

Although I was secretly pleased that we would not have to navigate our way through a humongous crowd, I felt a frisson of alarm as my brother and I alighted from the taxi. Had the rumor about the Rolling Stones been a hoax after all? I glanced at Alan. He seemed to be puzzled as well, and said, "Where is everyone? Are you sure this is the right place, Kath?" I reminded him that I had called the Phone Booth Club earlier, and had been told that the Rolling Stones were expected to show. As I spoke, pellets of sleet began bombarding our faces, and the two of us hustled towards the entrance. A sign outside the door confirmed that we were, indeed, about to enter the Phone Booth Club, and Alan reached for the door handle.

Suddenly, I remembered that I had no ID, and frantically tugged on his sleeve. "Hey! Wait a minute!" I cried. Alan glared at me, and I sheepishly confessed that my mind had been so focused on making it to the club, my underage status had completely slipped my mind. How the heck was I going to get inside when I had no legal proof of age, a slender figure—and the face of a fourteen-year-old? It was easy for my brother not to panic. After all, he was over eighteen, and his ID card was in his wallet.

Alan rolled his eyes and hissed, "You're telling me this *now?*"

My brother continued to mouth off at me as the two of us stood shivering on the sidewalk. I didn't blame him. Clearly, I was the one who owned the problem, and it was up to me to avoid getting carded at the club. I thought about how Mick and Keith might be hanging out on the other side of the door, and knew that I needed to devise a plan ASAP. I thought for a moment, and it dawned on me that I could masquerade as my brother's somewhat tipsy "date" for the evening. That way, the bouncer at the Phone Booth Club might hone in on him—and forget to check my ID. As soon as I explained my impromptu solution to Alan, a sickly expression suffused his face. For a moment, I thought he was going to ask me for a barf bag in response to my creepy request. Instead, he reluctantly agreed to put my plan into action. It didn't matter to me whether it had been the freezing wind or a secret hankering to rendezvous with the Rolling Stones that had persuaded him to give in so easily. I was grateful that he had agreed to cooperate, and continued to cling to him with a pseudo-tipsy demeanor as we entered the club.

Luckily, my little ruse seemed to work; the Maître d' approached us with a friendly smile. We checked our coats, and he waved Alan and me towards the lounge. I was pleased that this employee of the club had not suspected that I was an underage "Phone Booth Phony," and I slowly released the breath that I'd been holding.

Once my brother and I reached the bar, I promptly let go of his arm and sagged against the highly-polished countertop in relief. Alan signaled to the bartender and ordered a Black Russian for himself, and a 7&7 for me. As the two of us waited for our drinks to arrive, we took the opportunity to glance around the interior of the venue.

Chapter Two

The Phone Booth Club

From our vantage point, the Phone Booth Club appeared to be quite narrow, and alarmingly deserted. Besides Alan and me, there was only one other customer standing at the bar a bit further away from us. Several couples were huddled at tiny tables located near the back of the club, but the Maître d' was the only person in the foyer. It was still a mystery as to why the place was so empty . . .

Hadn't anyone else been listening to DJ Murray the K earlier that night?

And where the heck were the Rolling Stones?

As I continued to sip my drink, I began to wonder whether I would actually recognize members of the Rolling Stones if I saw them in person. Although their photographs were taped to my bedroom walls, I had only watched them on the Ed Sullivan show, and seen them perform several concerts at NYC's Academy of Music. What *would* members of the Rolling Stones look like up close (and personal!) minus all the fanfare and hype?

I glanced around, again, and noticed that the guy standing not too far from my brother and me seemed lost in thought. There was a rugged, almost brooding quality to his demeanor that was quite intriguing. As I continued to peek at him through the curtain of my wavy blonde hair, I scrutinized him further:

A longish face . . .

Sexy brown locks covering his eyebrows . . .

Slender build . . .

Stove-pipe trousers . . .

Dark-colored vest . . .

He had all the trademark *features* of rocker Keith Richards, and my heart began to hammer in my chest. I would have continued to stare at him with unabashed infatuation, but my brother was nudging me in the shoulder. I swiveled towards my sibling, and he announced that he was going to head on over to the men's room. As I watched him walk away, I smiled to myself. How convenient! While Alan was in the lavatory, I was going to be left alone at the bar with rock star Keith Richards of the Rolling Stones!

Once my brother had disappeared from view, I took another peek in the celebrity's direction. Without a Gibson guitar slung over his shoulder (or a mob of hysterical fans surrounding him), the slender young man dressed in tight pants, shirt, and vest could easily have been one of the guys hanging out at the local record shop. I couldn't help but notice that his complexion was slightly flawed and his countenance weary. He seemed a bit lonely, too; not at all like the celebrity my friends and I had watched rockin' away in concert at the Academy of Music.

A telephone rang somewhere near the front of the club. It jarred me out of my reverie, and served as a wake-up call that this was *the moment* to tell Keith Richards how much I adored his cool guitar riffs. Obviously, my brother would be returning from the rest room at any moment. Time was no longer on my side, so I took several steps in Vest-Man's direction and blurted out, "Are you Keith Richards?"

The instant the inane remark left my lips I blushed a crimson hue. Yikes! Why couldn't I have uttered a sultry "Hello there!" instead? At first, it seemed as though the Keith Richards look-alike had chosen to blatantly ignore my remark, but he slowly swiveled towards me. He flicked his long dark hair away from his eyes and hissed, "No, I'm not!" in a distinctly British accent. His words slammed me in the solar plexus as he turned away. I slinked back to contemplate my drink and pout in self-pity, but my "Rolling Stones Radar" kept insisting that this hip looking guy was rock star Keith Richards.

I glanced around the club in an attempt to regain what was left of my fragile composure, and saw that Alan had exited the men's room. It was clear that I had less than a minute to find another way to tell Keith Richards how much his music spoke to my soul. This time, I took a deep breath and announced in a voice just loud enough for him to hear, "Well, I think Keith's guitar solo on 'Heart of Stone' is really groovy, Man!" The guy standing nearby slowly swiveled back in my direction. He flashed me a boyish grin and said, "Thanks, Luv!" I smiled back at him, a look of triumph stretching across my face.

We both knew I had blown his cover!

Keith Richards opened his lips as if to say something more, but he suddenly clamped them shut and turned away as my brother arrived by my side. I took a final swig of my 7&7 and set the half-finished drink down on its coaster. The special moment with my fave-rave rock star had come to an end.

Alan picked up his glass and gulped down the remainder of his beverage. It was obvious that he hadn't recognized Keith Richards standing nearby (or seen me chatting with the rocker, either). My brother then leaned towards me, and said that we needed to split the scene, since it was getting late. Without waiting for my reply, he motioned for the bartender, and then paid for our drinks. I was reluctant to leave so soon, and suggested that we take a turn around the club before heading home. Luckily, Alan agreed, and the two of us ventured towards the back of the venue. As we sauntered away from the bar, I glanced back in Keith's direction. The invisible fortress he had seemingly erected around himself remained tightly in place. It was clear that he needed his space, so I decided to wait until later to tell Alan about my secret rendezvous with the famous guitarist.

While my brother and I headed towards the back of the club, I continued to bask in the after-glow of my private, tête-à-tête with

14

rocker Keith. I might have remained in this dreamy state for the rest of the night, except that bassist Bill Wyman of the Rolling Stones had suddenly appeared in my line of vision. He was seated at a semi-secluded table with his girlfriend Barbara (who I'd read about in various fan magazines) and I felt a fresh wave of anticipation. "Hey! Isn't that Bill Wyman over there?" I whispered in my brother's ear. Alan glanced in the direction I had indicated. He nodded his head, and the two of us picked up our pace. When we arrived by Bill Wyman's side, I was relieved to see that he and his companion were greeting us with friendly smiles. In fact, they were so welcoming and down-to-earth, I found myself blurting out, "You're Bill Wyman, aren't you?

It was clear that I had, once again, made a blunder by stating the obvious. I glanced away in embarrassment. Luckily, no one said a word, and the awkward moment quickly passed. "Yes, I am," the bassist replied in a silky tone of voice. His longish, wavy hair curled around his collar, and the wineglass he was holding glittered in the candlelight.

"Sorry to interrupt," I began anew, "But I wanted to tell you how much I dig your bass on 'The Last Time.'" As I spoke, Bill's glance raked my figure from the tips of my boobs to the toes of my black leather boots, and I blushed. When the bassist had finished giving me the once-over, he grinned at me.

"Glad you like it!" he replied.

My brother and I continued to converse with the rock star and his date for several more minutes, and I hung on Bill Wyman's every word. It was a privilege to hear him describe how he enjoyed composing creative riffs, and I complimented him several times on his far-out bass playing. My brother even joined in the conversation, too. As the four of us continued to chat, I found myself hankering for a memento of this special occasion. "May I have your autograph?" I asked the bassist. Bill Wyman nodded, and I began searching through my purse for a scrap of paper and a pen.

As I rummaged through the jumbled contents of my bag, I discovered that I had forgotten to bring any "meet-your-favorite-rock-star" supplies to the Phone Booth Club. Luckily, Bill's date had been poking through her handbag, too. I watched as she pulled a pen from its depths and tore off a corner from one of her shopping bags that was lying on a chair nearby. Her date then signed "Love, Bill Wyman—Stones" on the scrap of paper bag, and handed it to me. As I tucked the souvenir safely in my purse, Barbara told me to keep the pen. I thanked her, and said that I appreciated the time they had taken to speak with my brother and me.

"Yeah, we're sorry to have interrupted you like this . . ." Alan interjected.

"It's no trouble . . . really!" Bill Wyman insisted. He went on to say that he enjoyed meeting fans who truly appreciated his music, and I smiled back at him. Soon, Bill and his sweetheart said goodbye to Alan and me, and the two of us left their table. It had been heartwarming to learn that this famous musician was so open to meeting his fans, and I clutched my handbag containing his autograph tightly to my chest.

"Listen, Kathy!" my brother was saying. "I think we'd better head on home now."

"Aww! Can't we hang out here a little longer?" I cried. My brother slowly shook his head and rolled his eyes at me. Although he put on a good show of getting all huffy, I had a sneaking suspicion that he had enjoyed meeting Bill Wyman of the Rolling Stones, too.

"Well, I guess we can take a look around on our way out," Alan relented. "But remember . . ." I didn't hear the rest of his sentence; I was too busy making a bee-line towards a table near the front of the club, where I had spotted musician Brian Jones and his famous paramour, Anita Pallenberg. These fashion trendsetters were wearing matching white Edwardian-style blouses. Their blond hair was styled in similar unisex coifs, as well. I couldn't wait to meet this multi-instrumentalist from the Rolling Stones, and almost tripped over my feet as I approached the table where he and Anita were sitting. When I arrived by their side, Brian glanced up at me—and scowled. After my friendly chat with bassist Bill Wyman and his lady, I felt caught off-guard and began to back away.

"Oh! Great! Another round of rock-star-rudeness," I muttered under my breath as my brother arrived by my side. Although I could understand how celebrities might become irritated with fans constantly mobbing them for their autographs, the Phone Booth Club was virtually empty. "Why can't Brian Jones take two seconds out of his evening to scribble his name on a piece of paper for me?" I wondered.

I could have walked away after encountering Brian's harsh rebuttal.

Instead, I mustered up my courage, again, and took several steps *towards* him. After apologizing politely, I asked whether he would give me his autograph. My brother waited patiently next to me while Brian seemed to take forever to consider my request. Finally, the musician nodded his head, and relief flooded through me. I scooped up a Phone Booth tent card that was lying in the middle of the table, and retrieved Barbara's pen from my purse. After handing Brian both of these items, he wrote his name on the card, and I took the opportunity to tell him how much I enjoyed his guitar and harmonica playing. "Ta, Luv," he replied.

The multi-instrumentalist handed me his autograph. He then cocked his head to one side, and stared at me with a quizzical expression on his face. The way he was studying me made me wonder whether it was unusual for female fans to make remarks about his musical prowess. No doubt the majority of chicks were more interested in finding out whether he *made great music* in bed.

As I tucked the card with his autograph into my handbag, I longed to say something more. However, Anita must have been anticipating that I'd try and prolong the encounter. She leaned towards her lover with an enticing view of her ample cleavage and, soon, they were engaged in a very heavy kiss. Her not-so-subtle message had been crystal clear, and my brother and I promptly turned away from their table.

On our way out, Alan and I passed by the bar. Keith Richards was nowhere in sight, and I was disappointed that he had managed to slip away. "I'll see you again," I whispered to the spot where he and I had chatted earlier. By the time we arrived in the vestibule, a crowd of patrons had gathered there. Many people were lined up outside, waiting to get into the club, as well. It was obvious that Alan and I had been so focused on speaking with Brian Jones, we had been oblivious to the fact that the Phone Booth Club had started to fill up.

What if Mick Jagger showed up two minutes after we had left the venue? And . . . maybe drummer Charlie Watts was on his way to the club, as well! I longed to turn around, grab a table, and join the partygoers hustling in the opposite direction. However, I also knew that the ambiance inside the night spot was rapidly changing. The rock stars I had met earlier would soon be surrounded by a bevy of fans, and might no longer be so accessible. I needed to get a grip . . . needed to be grateful that I had already met Keith Richards, Bill Wyman, and Brian Jones on a one-on-one basis.

By then, it was almost midnight. Alan and I were already late getting home, and my brother must have been feeling a lot of parental pressure by that point in time. Despite the age-old double standard that I had bitched about earlier, in reality, I would not have made it to the Phone Booth Club had my sibling not escorted me there. Once I had put things into perspective, I willingly followed my brother to the coat check, and then the front door. Stepping outside, we were pummeled by the wintery wind. But I didn't mind. Instead, my soul was chanting "I can't believe we met the Stones!" over and over while I danced an impromptu jig en route to the curb.

I was still floating on a make-believe cloud as Alan hustled the two of us into the cab that he had flagged down for our return trip home. Once we had settled back against the squabs, my mind began a mental replay of the evening:

> "Murray the K's" radio rumor . . . Alan's cleaning ultimatum . . . my ID dilemma . . . unmasking rocker Keith Richards . . . Bill Wyman's friendly demeanor . . . Brian Jones and Anita Pallenberg . . . Bill and Brian's autographs tucked safely away in my purse . . .

"Earth to Kathy! Earth to Kathy!" I heard my brother calling as if from miles away. At the sound of his voice, I slammed back to reality—and the cab's dimly lit interior. "It was great meeting Brian and Bill, but I wonder why Mick and Keith didn't show?" he was saying. I glanced out the window. Thick flakes of snow were now tumbling from the sky. I slowly turned back towards my brother, and squirmed in my seat.

"Well, actually . . . I spoke with Keith when you were in the john," I replied. Alan stared at me, his jaw sagging down towards his shoulders.

"You mean the guy standing near us at the bar was Keith Richards?"

"Yup!" I replied with a grin.

"I sure picked the wrong time to pee!" he huffed. I giggled, and said that I was glad the Phone Booth Club had been so empty when we arrived. That way we were able to have special time with the Rolling Stones.

"Thanks again for taking me, Alan. I'll never forget tonight!" My brother shook his head at me.

"Yeah . . . well you'd better start remembering it, because meeting the Stones was a once-in-a-lifetime experience."

I glanced out the window again.

"That's what you think!" I muttered under my breath as the cab sped through the streets towards Central Park.

Chapter Three

The Broad
With the Braids

I kept the autographs of Bill Wyman and Brian Jones safely tucked away in my lingerie drawer for the next year and a half as waves of the psychedelic scene rippled eastward from San Francisco and arrived in New York. Rock 'n' roll was all the rage, but my life had already reached a turning point the night I met members of the Rolling Stones. By the Spring of 1967 I was a diehard Anglophile attending New York City's Lehman College, and the proud owner of a round-trip ticket for a European summer vacation to France, Scandinavia and Great Britain. I was antsy for the semester to end so I could launch the "Bushnell Invasion of Britain" and scout the streets of London for rock 'n' roll icons from my Flower Power generation.

In addition to the Rolling Stones and Beatles, I spent hours grooving on a plethora of other groups and solo artists, including:

Bob Dylan, Cream, the Who, Led Zeppelin, the Animals, Buffalo Springfield, the Kinks, the Yardbirds, Jimi Hendrix, Jefferson Airplane, the Doors, the Byrds, Simon and Garfunkel, Joan Baez, Donovan, the Moody Blues, Procol Harum, the Hollies, as well as Linda Ronstadt, Janis Joplin, the Lovin' Spoonful, Crosby, Stills, and Nash, and bluesman John Mayall.

Friends of mine also turned me on to the bands Quicksilver Messenger Service, Love, the Rascals, the Velvet Underground, Pearls Before Swine, and the Chain Reaction.

I flew the Union Jack from my fire escape window. My father had taught me various chords on the family guitar, and I purchased a sequined shoulder strap for it. Each day when I arrived home from my college classes, I slung the instrument over my shoulder, and would strut around my bedroom all decked out and ready to rock! I secretly longed for a legendary Les Paul guitar, and the strength in my slender fingers to master the powerful bar chords that my male musician idols played with ease.

Then there were other times when I'd discard the rock star stance, sublimate my "dick-for-a-day" desire, and adopt a copy-cat version of the latest girlie teeny-bopper gear. I would iron my hair, and parade around my room pretending that I was British fashion paragon Jean Shrimpton. Less than a week later, I'd drop the super-model routine, rig up a make-shift microphone stand from a mop handle, and strut-my-stuff, once again, as lead guitarist of my fantasy rock band.

In-between classical piano lessons, ballet classes at Joffrey's, a part-time job, and midterm exams, I continued to write songs of my own. I also managed to squeeze in enough time to browse through the local bookstores and travel agencies, searching for the latest European pamphlets and guides. Soon, I had amassed a credible collection of tourist information, and was basking in the sweet anticipation of my upcoming summer trip.

My joy was short-lived, however, when Mom and Dad suddenly came up with a real downer by announcing that I was not allowed to travel on my European excursion unless I was accompanied by a female companion. Once I had recovered from this latest parental bombshell, I dutifully spent the next several weeks asking my female friends whether they would be able to go with me on the trip. Unfortunately, my buddies didn't have the extra money. I wasn't exactly padded in the pocket myself (just my bras!) but had somehow managed to scrape up enough for the plane ticket and a cache of British Sterling.

Why was it so difficult to locate another die-hard Anglophile who had some money stashed away?

And where were all the female rock 'n' roll fanatics willing to trash their Fred Braun shoes while trekking around the streets of London?

By mid-May I still had not found a travel mate. The Lehman College Summer trip was less than a month away, and I sat moaning to myself in the campus cafeteria while pondering my dilemma. What the heck did my parents expect me to do? Put an ad in *The New York Times* for a travel companion? I scooped up my textbooks into a tidy pile, and was just about to grab my purse when I spotted my brother, who was also attending Lehman College. Alan was wending his way through the throng of students towards me, and I waved to him.

"Hey! What's up?" my sibling asked as he hunkered down beside me in a vacant chair.

"I'm up shit's creek—that's what!" I replied with a groan. "Mom and Dad are threatening to cancel my summer plane reservation 'cause I still haven't found a chick who's able to travel with me to Europe."

"So, what's the big deal? There has to be hundreds of other Keith Richards fanatics running around the planet," he replied. I stared back at him and sighed. It was obvious why my parents might be concerned about my safety (or that I'd succumb to the charms of some foreign Fabian), but they were certainly not making it easy for me to go on my upcoming, summer trip.

"I still don't see why a girl can't go on vacation alone if she wants to . . ." I began. My brother shrugged his shoulders, and I leaned back in my chair. "Oh, Alan! You're so lucky to be a guy and not have all these lousy restrictions." My sibling glared at me.

"Listen! If this conversation's going to turn into another one of your 'It's-A-Man's-World' sob stories, I'm outta here," he growled.

"Look! I can't always follow the family rules like a good little lemming. My plane ticket's non-refundable, and *nothing's* gonna stop me from going on the trip. You dig?"

As I spoke, my brother must have, indeed, dug into his memory-bank, and dredged up the recollection of freezing his fanny outside the Phone Booth Club. He shook his head, rolled his eyes, and muttered something under his breath. The two of us sat in silence for the next, several minutes. During this time, I noticed that a dozen or so students had arrived at a nearby table. They were dressed in an array of colorful clothing accessorized with a variety of beads, bandannas, and jingly bells. It was obvious that these young men and women were members of Lehman's burgeoning Hippie clique. As I scrutinized them further, one young woman in particular seemed to stand out from the crowd. She was wearing a Day-Glo blue shawl draped decorously over her calf-length dress. Her dark brown hair was parted into two thick braids, and a wide-brimmed hat was perched on her head at a jaunty angle. Shoulder-length, beaded earrings swayed across the nape of her neck as she stooped to take a seat. I found myself intrigued by this young woman, and I pointed discreetly in her direction. Alan glanced over at her table. I leaned towards him and whispered, "Who's that chick over there?"

"If you're talking about the broad with the braids, I think her name's Janet," he replied. He went on to say something else but, by then, I was shamelessly eavesdropping on the conversation taking place between the charismatic chick named Janet and her cronies.

". . . but all my friends seem to be going to Spain and Italy instead of Scandinavia and London," I heard her saying. Woah! It sounded as though Janet and I shared similar travel itineraries! I scooped up my textbooks and purse, and raced over to her table.

"Excuse me, but . . . um . . . I couldn't help overhearing what you said about going to London," I stammered. "Were you referring to the Lehman summer trip to Europe by any chance?" The young woman glanced up. Her eyes were bugging out like a black Mollie fish. She nodded, but continued to stare at me. I began explaining that I had been searching for another female who was traveling to Scandinavia and London on the Lehman summer trip. Janet still did not reply, and I promptly launched into a verbal rendition of my travel itinerary. By the time I had finished, this enigmatic Hippie chick had seemingly regained her composure, and was smiling at me.

"This is incredible!" Janet said. She went on to explain that she had been searching for what seemed like ages, hoping to find a female travel companion interested in going to the same places she wanted to see. "And all of a sudden you show up out of the blue like this!" she exclaimed. Janet tugged her shawl more tightly around her shoulders, while I hunkered down on the seat next to her. A slew of goose bumps had formed along my arms, and I tried to swipe them away.

"Shit, man! Talk about fate . . ." I muttered.

"I can't believe it, either!" Janet leaned towards me, and gave my hands a friendly squeeze. "You know, this has got to be the only time in my life that I'm glad someone eavesdropped on me!" she quipped.

Once our laughter had died down, we formally introduced ourselves, and then my new friend gave me a run-down regarding the itinerary for her summer trip. This included spending several days soaking up the sights of Paris before departing for Scandinavia. After that, she planned to take a boat across the North Sea to Edinburgh, and then make her way to London. As she spoke, I heard my brother calling out to me. I was having so much fun talking travel with this chick, that my fanny remained rooted to the spot—and I shook my head at him. I quickly turned my attention back to my new acquaintance, and told her that I'd been wanting to get to London ever since I saw the Beatles on the Ed Sullivan Show. As we continued to chat, I wondered whether Janet preferred the Rolling Stones, or if she was a die-hard Beatles fan.

I was just about to ask her whether she had a preference between the two bands, when the clanging of a bell echoed throughout the cafeteria. It signaled the next change of classes, and I stood up and glanced at my brother's table. His seat was now empty, and I turned my attention back to Janet. "Listen," she was saying, "I have an English class this period. Why don't you give me your number and I'll call you this evening so we can discuss our plans in more detail?" She slid a pen and spiral notebook towards me, and I scribbled down my contact information (along with a goofy "smiley face").

"Honey, I think you already had my number—long before I gave it to you!" I replied with a chuckle.

Janet telephoned me later that day, and we spent over an hour discussing various travel itineraries. During the conversation, we also chatted about our favorite rock bands, and she asked whether I'd seen the Beatles perform at Shea Stadium. I explained that my brother and I had managed to score a couple of tickets to this event, but our seats were in the upper deck. The stage was so friggin' far away, the Mop Tops looked like a bunch of tiny toothpicks from where we were sitting.

"Apparently, the crowd was screaming so loudly the Beatles couldn't even hear themselves play," Janet remarked. I told her that my brother and I could hear them a bit, but I had also spotted through my binoculars two guys that looked like Mick and Keith who were seated in the box behind home plate. All the fans were so busy screaming their lungs out over John and Paul, it seemed like nobody was paying much attention to the fact that the Stones were there, too. I also ended up telling Janet how I had met musicians Keith Richards, Bill Wyman, and Brian Jones at the Phone Booth Club.

"But I want you to know that I have no intention of ever becoming a groupie," I added.

"Phew! That's a relief . . . because I'm not into that ASS-pect of the scene, either," Janet chortled. I was glad to hear that she had taken a similar (non-horizontal) position regarding rock stars, but hoped that she wasn't opposed to engaging in lengthy discussions about hunky, fantasy men.

The following afternoon Janet and I met in the college cafeteria in order to finalize our plans for the summer. As we poured over our numerous brochures and travel guides, it became clear that we both wanted to spend the majority of our frugal vacation in Great Britain. So, we decided to book our London stay at Mrs. Zurita's Guest House, an affordable B&B in the suburb of Clapham Common. Once the two of us had finished compiling our wish list of enticing travel activities, we found ourselves chatting, once again, about the various groups that we grooved on in the rock music scene.

"It seems like I've been to a zillion shows here in New York," I remarked. "I've seen the Byrds, the Mamas and the Papas, the Animals . . . you name it! I even saw the Fugs play at some club on MacDougal Street in Greenwich Village. Their singer sure lived up to his wild-man reputation when he ran through the audience screaming, 'Kill for Peace!'"

"With an act like that, I'll bet they didn't need a light show!" Janet remarked with a chuckle. "Was their volume as outrageous as their lyrics?"

"Nah! We're not talking Blue Cheer!" I replied. I went on to tell her that my brother's friend, Michael Kamen, and his band Emil and the Detectives had played at my family's apartment for my birthday the previous year. They had actually finished two entire sets in our living room before the neighbors called the cops. Janet chuckled, and said that she didn't think her parents would allow a rock group to play in their home. "Well, that's one of the coolest things my Mom and Dad ever let me do," I replied.

"Just because a rock band's loud doesn't necessarily mean it's better," Janet pointed out. I nodded, and told her that I thought that Jim McGuinn and his band, the Byrds, had a dynamite way of getting their message across—without blasting everyone's eardrums off the planet. The two of us began discussing the song "Eight Miles High," and we both agreed that it was a drag that radio stations were banning the track just because the lyrics were supposedly perverting the minds of *innocent* adolescents.

"What I don't understand is why the media blatantly ignores corruption in our government, and chooses to focus on censoring a bunch of harmless rock 'n' roll lyrics, instead," I remarked.

"Don't get me started!" Janet replied with a sigh.

Chapter Four

Feather Man
& Savoy Brown

After traveling to France via TWA, Janet and I checked in at L'Hotel D'Harcourt that was located at 3 Boulevard St-Michel on the Left Bank of Paris. We then spent a whirlwind week of sightseeing, including trekking around the streets of Paris, visiting the Eiffel Tower, L'Arc de Triomphe, and ogling the masterpieces in the Louvre. My friend and I also hung out at Monmartre, toured Notre Dame and Versailles, putting our college French to the test while chatting with various patrons at the local cafes.

In a quirky twist of fate, I ended up going on a casual dinner date with a French "Fabian," after all—a handsome jeweler who had a kiosk near our hotel on the Left Bank. After the meal, we strolled along the cobblestones near the Seine in the moonlight, and he asked me in rapid-fire French whether I would live with him in Paris (at least that's what I *thought* he said). I shook my head in reply. After all, I was only eighteen—a rock 'n' roll Anglophile headed for Copenhagen on my way to London. The jeweler's footsteps slowed as he walked me to my lodgings. He gave me a quick peck on the cheek, and I watched as he headed towards the nearest Metro station.

Janet and I were reluctant to depart the rich historical ambiance, lovely parks, winding streets, and yummy pastries of the City of Lights the following morning. With the help of our Eurail Passes, we boarded a train bound for Copenhagen. En route, she and I gazed at the scenic Scandinavian countryside, and marveled at our new-found sense of independence, as well. By the time we had checked into a local Youth Hostel near the famous Tivoli Gardens, the French jeweler and the Louvre seemed far away.

The following morning, Janet and I made the rounds of several tourist destinations, including the Little Mermaid and Kastellet. Later, as we were window-shopping, the scent of incense and the enticing sound of guitars wafted towards us from a nearby park. We headed in that direction, and soon discovered that a Danish Hippie celebration was in progress. As we wandered through the gathering, we basked in the sunshine that was streaming down on the young men and women dressed in their colorful, flowing garments. We passed by several people dancing in a circle, and stopped briefly to listen to a guy who was stretched out on a bench strumming a guitar. Patchouli scented incense and the notes of a flute were wafting in the breeze while we made our way deeper into the crowd.

Although the atmosphere was festive, I had attended a Be-In at the Sheep Meadow in New York City's Central Park—where thousands of Hippies had gathered. Having experienced such a massive Peace, Love, and Flower-Power gathering as this, the one in Copenhagen seemed rather tame in comparison. Janet must have felt the difference, too. She turned towards me and chuckled. "This 'happening' isn't really happening is it?" I grinned, and said that it certainly was not like the ones I had attended at the Sheep Meadow in Central Park. Janet suggested that we split the scene, and check out the rest of the park. I concurred, and we headed towards the outskirts of the celebration, where the crowd had thinned out considerably.

Most of the Hippies at the Danish celebration had been dressed in an array of psychedelic colors, bell-bottom jeans and long, flowing dresses. However, it was the guy walking directly in front of us wearing an elaborately-embroidered caftan and headband with a giant feather poking out of it who had grabbed our attention. He was quite thin with wispy brown hair. The way he seemed to be gliding along the sidewalk lent an almost ethereal quality to his gait. Janet must have been curious about this mysterious guy as well.

"Hey! Check out that cat over there," she whispered in my ear. I giggled, and soon, the two of us had caught up with him. Suddenly, the young man swiveled around in our direction, and I nearly bumped into him. The feather in his headband was waving in the breeze while he smiled at my friend and me.

"Hello there!" he greeted us with a distinctly British accent. The stranger's inflection reminded me of Bill Wyman, the Beatles, and the fact that I couldn't wait to check out the British music scene (and the latest gear on Carnaby Street). "If you girls need a place to stay in London, you're welcome to crash at my flat on Holland Park Avenue," he added. I took a step back as a tingling sensation began to creep up along my spine. How the heck did this stranger know that my friend and I were on our way to London?

Janet glanced at me. Her mouth was open, too, as if to ask, "Is this guy for real?" Before either of us had a chance to reply, the young man introduced himself as Martin Stone. He was a guitarist for the Savoy Brown Blues Band that was based in Britain. As he spoke, his vocal intonation was as soft as the feather that adorned his headband. I leaned forward in an attempt to catch his every syllable, and noticed that Janet was straining to hear him, too. After we told him our names, he asked whether we would be interested in attending a gig his band was playing later that evening. The notion of seeing Savoy Brown was quite alluring, and I was secretly pleased when Janet nodded her head.

"Sure! I'm up for it! How 'bout you, Kath?"

"SOUNDS good to me!" I replied. Janet rolled her eyes at my obnoxious pun, while the guitarist stifled a smile. Martin suggested that we meet with him later that evening, so we could ride with his band to the gig. My friend nodded, and began rummaging through her woven bag. She pulled out her address book and a pen, and handed them to our new acquaintance. Feather Man wrote down the address of his flat in London, and the location of his Copenhagen lodgings where his band was staying. He also told us the time that we should rendezvous with him later that evening. Janet tucked her address book and pen back into her bag, and the three of us smiled at one another.

"Then, I'll see you chicks later," the guitarist confirmed before he waved goodbye. As he walked away, the feather in his headband was still bobbing in the breeze. My friend and I remained rooted to the spot, still wondering how the heck this guy named Martin Stone had known that we were on our way to Britain.

"It's not like we have 'Jet-Setting-to-London' tattooed on our foreheads, or anything,' I muttered.

"Well, today's been so totally freaky, I wonder what tonight's going to be like . . ." Janet mused.

Although we had both expected to see an assortment of groupie chicks hanging out at Savoy Brown's Copenhagen digs later that evening, when we arrived, the only other females present were a buxom blonde and her younger sister. Martin greeted us at the door, and led us inside. He then began introducing us to the members of his band. First, we shook hands with Kim Simmonds, a blond-haired guitarist and founding member of Savoy Brown. I noticed that one of the Danish sisters was clinging to his arm. Next, we met the band's vocalist, a friendly guy named Brice Portius. Several minutes later we were introduced to drummer Leo Manning, and a red-headed bassist (with mutton-chops) called Ray Chappell. As Martin's bandmates smiled at Janet and me, I secretly hoped that none of them had assumed that we were groupie chicks.

There was only time for a quick "cuppa" tea before the roadie announced that it was time for Savoy Brown to depart for its gig. As everyone headed towards the van, Martin assured Janet and me that the band's equipment had been set up earlier at the club. So, there should be plenty of room for everyone to ride in the vehicle. Unfortunately, he forgot to mention that there were only two seats in the van—which meant that the only place left to sit was on the filthy, metal floor. As I surveyed the masses of empty candy wrappers and cigarette butts that were scattered around, I wondered whether I would be able to find a relatively clean spot in which to park my tush.

"Make yourselves at home, ladies!" one of the band members quipped while Janet and I were squishing ourselves in-between Martin and Ray. Raucous laughter erupted throughout the vehicle after this remark, but I didn't join in the reverie; I was too preoccupied trying to prevent myself from toppling over onto Ray's lap as the van pulled away from the curb.

En route to the club, the interior of the van was rapidly becoming darker by the minute. I glanced up at the windows, and saw that dusk had fallen. The streetlights we passed were whizzing by so fast, it created a strobe-like effect throughout the interior of the vehicle. Various slurping sounds could be heard in a far corner, as well. It was obvious that Kim and his willowy blonde were into some heavy petting. In the meantime, bassist Ray was asking Janet and me whether we had been to Denmark before. His nonchalant, vocal intonation made it seem as though he was oblivious to the sexual activity unfolding in the back of the van. "Nope! This is our first time in Europe," I announced in-between Kim's intermittent moans. Janet and I began giving Ray a run-down on our travel itinerary, but the van soon pulled up outside the club where Savoy Brown had been booked for its gig. The driver deftly parked the vehicle, and I gathered up my purse (while Kim and his chick rearranged their disheveled attire).

After alighting from the vehicle, Janet and I followed Savoy Brown into the club, and then further inside, towards the backstage area. Several groupies were hanging around outside the dressing room. They scowled at Janet and me as we made our way inside the band's private domain. As soon as the door closed behind us, several members of Savoy Brown began changing their clothes. I glanced at Janet. Her eyebrows were raised upwards, as if to question whether we should remain in the dressing room—especially since we weren't Savoy Brown's groupie chicks.

"Listen you guys! Janet and I are going to head for the loo," I announced to no one in particular. As my friend and I made our way out of the backstage area, I chided myself for being such a naïve, uptight chick. Janet took one look at my ruffled demeanor and began to laugh.

"Looks like we need to get used to these changing-room scenarios," she quipped as the two of us headed towards the ladies' room. We hung out in the grimy lavatory for a while, but it was rapidly filling up with groupies vying for a spot at the mirror. So we exited the loo, walking towards the stage. A crowd had already gathered there, and we picked up our pace while making our way through the throng. Luckily, we were able to secure two spots that would give us an excellent view of the show. When members of Savoy Brown rushed onstage several minutes later, vocalist Brice stepped up to the microphone. Soon, he was belting out the lyrics, while Martin and Kim battled it out on lead guitar. I grooved on Kim's harmonica solos, as well, and vowed to myself that I'd be able to play a mean blues harp myself, one day.

After their gig, members of Savoy Brown invited us to attend a private get-together that was being held at a home on the outskirts of Copenhagen. By the time we arrived there, numerous friends of the band were already on the scene. As the two of us wandered around the party, the song "Tales of Brave Ulysses" by the band Cream was blasting from the record player. When the track ended, Savoy Brown's bassist, Ray, shouted at a young man sitting next to the phonograph to play the song again. After that, Ray kept requesting that "Tales of Brave Ulysses" be played again . . . and then again. Soon, I had lost count of the number of times this particular track had rotated around the turntable.

"I really dig this song, but if I hear it one more time . . ." I whispered in Janet's ear.

"Yeah, it definitely loses something in the loop, doesn't it," my friend snickered. As she spoke, Feather Man wandered over to us with a glass of wine in his hand. He asked us whether we wanted a sip, but didn't wait for our reply. Instead, he went on to inform us that he had just "dropped a tab" of LSD. I glanced around the room and sighed. Was everyone at the party tripping out on acid except for the traveling American Chicks?

After several hours of non-stop partying, many of the young men and women began to nod out. I curled up on the floor, as well, and finally fell asleep. By the time I awoke from my fitful slumber, dawn was just beginning to break. At some point during the night, Ray had finally relinquished control of the phonograph and was slumped up against a chair. Other partygoers had crashed out, too. It was clear that most everyone around us was tripping or soused, and I wondered how Janet and I were going to get a ride back to the youth hostel.

I glanced around, again, and saw that Martin was huddled on a nearby chair. After crawling over to him, I asked whether Savoy Brown's roadie would give Janet and me a lift back to our lodgings. Feather-Man regarded me with a far-away look in his eyes; I wasn't even sure if he was aware of my presence. So, I returned to my little niche on the floor and hunkered down, once again. When I awoke several hours later, sunlight was streaming through the curtains onto the hardwood floor. I slowly sat up and glanced around the room. From my vantage point, I noticed that the majority of Hippies were still crashed out, oblivious to the fact that guitarist Kim was groping his girlfriend on a couch across the room. Despite being fully clothed, their bodies were undulating in a decidedly sexual manner. Suddenly, Kim jumped up from the couch and hustled over to his roadie. Soon, he had the keys to the van in his hand. I smiled to myself. After all, it seemed likely that he and his lover would "christen" the back of the vehicle before anyone discovered their hideaway.

Not long after Kim and his chick had split the scene, Janet awoke. She stretched her arms over her head and muttered, "What time is it, Kath?"

"It's time to get the hell out of here," I replied with a smirk.

"Isn't it a bit late to bitch about being stranded?" she muttered. Janet glanced around the room. It was obvious that Kim and his girlfriend were nowhere in sight, and I explained that the guitarist was probably screwing his chick out in the van. When Janet heard this, she began to chuckle. Soon, the two of us were laughing so loudly that we woke up several people who were stretched out on the floor nearby. Once our raucous outburst had died down a bit, I stood up, and stretched my arms. At the same time, Ray was making his way over to the record player. It wasn't long before melodic strains of "A Whiter Shade of Pale" by Procol Harum were wafting through the house. As I began humming along with the lyrics, it occurred to me that I must have looked a bit *pale*, myself—and I wondered whether I'd ever get in the groove of these wild party nights.

Chapter Five

Derek and the UFO Club

When Janet and I arrived in London, we immersed ourselves in many of the tourist activities. We rode on the top of the iconic double-decker buses, teased the guards at Buckingham Palace, checked out Carnaby Street, Speaker's Corner, the British Museum, Piccadilly Circus, and hung out with the locals near the fountains at Trafalgar Square. Although we had Martin's London address in our luggage, we took up residence as planned in Mrs. Zurita's Guest House, a B&B in Clapham Common on the southern outskirts of London.

During our various sightseeing forays into the City, Janet and I joked around about how we were hoping to bump into the Beatles (or see one of the Hollies standing at a bus stop!). However, we obviously didn't spot any rock 'n' roll icons hanging out at any of these places. By then, we were beginning to tire of the lengthy commute back and forth from Clapham Common to the center of the city. After one busy day admiring the masterpieces at the National Gallery, and then dinner at a nearby eatery, it had been growing late. On our way back to the B&B, we were crammed in the carriage of a tube train, clutching the safety bars as it rumbled along a tunnel under the Thames towards our outpost lodgings.

"Why don't we check out Feather Man's place in the next couple of days?" Janet suggested. I nodded in agreement and, suddenly the train lurched as it rounded a curve. I nearly lost my grip on the safely pole, and barely avoided tumbling into the lap of the guy sitting near me. As I muttered a half-assed apology in his direction, he nodded at me, and I took another peek at him. I'm not sure whether it was because I had just seen all of the dreamy paintings at the National Gallery that afternoon or what . . . but the young man's Renaissance-style hair, finely sculpted face, and smattering of freckles across the bridge of his nose reminded me of a Botticelli painting. So did the bright yellow daffodil he was removing from a buttonhole in his shirt, and handing up at me.

"For me?" I blurted out. Botticelli Boy nodded, and tucked the flower in my hand. I raised the daffodil to my nose as the Tube train pulled into Clapham Common Station.

"Come on, Kath!" Janet called out. She grabbed my arm, the doors slid open, and we maneuvered our way out of the train and onto the platform. Although the daffodil was a bit crushed by then, I had still managed to hold on to it.

"Whew! How come the Tube's so jam-packed this late at night?" I groaned.

"And how come you're holding that flower in your hand?" my friend wanted to know. I explained to her about the guy who had given it to me, and she said that she remembered him. Suddenly, Janet pointed upwards and said, "Oh! Look! There he is! See? Up there ahead of us on the escalator." I glanced in that direction, and saw that the young man who had given me the daffodil was riding up the moving staircase. Janet and I hopped on the escalator, as well, and I found myself wondering if he lived in the Clapham Common area.

My friend and I had walked less than a block towards the B&B where we were staying, when I felt a tugging sensation on my sleeve. I motioned for the two of us to stop, whirled around—and came face-to-face with Botticelli Boy. "Ello girls," he announced with a friendly Cockney drawl. "Like the flower, then?" I fidgeted with the daffodil in my hand and nodded. "You chicks been to the UFO Club yet?"

"The what . . . ?" Janet asked. The young guy told us that it was a cool, psychedelic rock club on Tottenham Court Road. He went on to say that his name was Derek, and that the UFO Club was open all night long. Janet glanced over at me; I could tell that the mention of live rock music had piqued her interest, too. We both listened closely as Derek told us more about the club, and then he confessed that his parents had thrown him out of the house that day.

"I was planning to sleep on a bench somewhere on Clapham Common but . . ." he trailed off.

"Oh, no! You can't do that!" I insisted.

"So, you birds want to check out the UFO Club with me, instead?" Janet and I couldn't resist. Soon, the three of us had returned to the Tube station, and we were riding the Underground back towards Central London.

Once the bouncer checked Derek's UFO Membership at the entrance to the club, Janet and I paid the fee for the three of us and we followed our new friend down a steep flight of stairs. As we approached the bottom of the stairwell, the live music grew increasingly louder. Flashing strobe lights and incense greeted our senses, while we made our way past the stage. I glanced around, and saw that members of the rock band performing were silhouetted against a backdrop of amoeba-like shapes that were slithering around on a screen behind them. These colorful blobs were pulsating in time to the eerie, electronic instrumental that the group was playing.

"Who's that band?" I shouted in Derek's direction.

"It's not the Who, you twit! It's Pink Floyd," he hissed in my ear. I made a mental note of the band's name, and glanced again at the curly-headed lead guitarist with his brooding aura (and intriguing solo notes) before turning around and following Janet and Derek towards the back of the club. As the three of us made our way through the crowd, we were careful not to stumble over the patrons who were sprawled out on the floor. We also made sure to give a wide berth to those who were flailing their arms as they danced around in wild abandon. Once Derek finally found a space large enough for the three of us to squeeze into, we hunkered down on the grungy floor. I sat down cross legged next to my friends and closed my eyes. Soon, I was picturing myself standing center stage, rockin' out on lead guitar with Pink Floyd—and the song we were playing was outta sight.

I continued to savor the mental image for several more minutes, and then I finally opened my eyes. Janet was smiling at me and several seconds later, Derek leaned towards the two of us. Once Botticelli Boy had our full attention, he informed us that we'd better make ourselves comfortable. The Underground had closed, and we were going to be spending the night at the UFO Club. Janet opened her mouth as if to reply, but the DJ had put the Beatles track "All You Need Is Love," on the turntable. Suddenly, the crowd of UFO patrons began dancing together in time to the music. Janet and I became caught up in the moment, as well. We stood up and began swaying to the hypnotic beat. Soon, everyone in the club seemed to be singing along with the Beatle's track "All You Need Is Love" as it blasted out over the PA system.

Next, members of a group called the Bonzo Dog Doo-Dah Band took the stage and, later, the Crazy World of Arthur Brown began its performance. I rose up on my tiptoes just in time to see a guy attached to a pulley "fly" out from the wings. He was wearing a helmet that was spouting actual flames as he belted out the lyrics to his song, "Fire! Let It Burn!" I watched as the flamboyant singer landed center-stage. He continued to strut around in his flaming attire while the crowd egged him on. I personally would have preferred that Pink Floyd return to the stage . . . but kept my opinion to myself as the crowd continued their Arthur Brown fire-fueled frenzy.

Janet must have been thinking along the same lines; she leaned over and shouted in my ear, "Frankly, Kath, I'd rather have the Doors light my fire any day."

Chapter Six

A Harp Lesson With Botticelli Boy

When I awoke the following morning on the floor of the UFO Club, a shaft of pale sunlight was filtering down the stairwell. Nearly everyone had split the scene, the stage was empty, and the premises littered with trash. A tattered copy of the *International Times* was scattered on the floor next to me. Janet sat up, too, and stretched her arms. I leaned over and playfully poked Derek's sleeping form. He slowly sat up, rubbed his bleary eyes, and asked whether Janet and I wanted to go for a bite to eat.

"Nah, I think I'll head back to Mrs. Z's and get some ZZ's," Janet quipped.

"Are you sure?" I asked her. My travel buddy nodded and rose to her feet. Derek and I followed her and, soon, the three of us were heading up the steep staircase towards the exit. After we had navigated around several garbage men who were gathering trash outside the club, Janet waved good-bye to Derek and me. We watched as she headed towards the Tottenham Court Road Tube station. I felt a bit guilty that I had not volunteered to accompany her back to our B&B lodgings, but my stomach was rumbling, so I tagged alongside Derek as he made his way towards a nearby café.

After an English breakfast of beans on toast and a cup of tea, we left the café and began walking down the street. As the two of us strolled along, Derek pulled a blues harmonica out of his pocket and began playing a series of complex, wailing notes that sailed through the early morning air. I had always admired the way Mick Jagger played harmonica on the songs "Little Red Rooster" and "Look What You've Done." I'd also been inspired by guitarist Kim Simmonds when I heard him play harmonica solos at Savoy Brown's Copenhagen gig. So inspired, in fact, that I had vowed to learn how to play a mean blues harp—and add that sound to some of the songs I'd been writing. Maybe Derek would teach me how to play. It was worth a try, wasn't it? I grabbed his arm, and we slowed our steps.

"Hey! Where'd you learn to play like that?" I asked. Botticelli Boy shoved the instrument back into his pocket, and explained that there really was nothing to it. He'd simply listened to lots of blues records, and copied what the harmonica players were doing. "Well, you sure play a mean harp, man! Will you teach me how to get that sound?"

Derek stared at me and said, "Oh, come on, Luv! You can't be serious. Chicks don't play 'arp."

"Well, I'm *seriously* interested!"

Derek rolled his eyes, and reluctantly pulled the shiny instrument from his jeans pocket. After wiping the front of it on his sleeve, he handed it to me. As soon as I blew into it, an atrocious, honking noise blasted through the air. "Ugh! I can't get a decent sound out of this thing." My new blues harp instructor reached over, took the instrument from me, and cracked a smile.

"It's easy! All you have to do is blow and suck."

"Are you getting fresh with me?" I teased. Derek muttered something under his breath, but then he grinned at me again.

"Here! I'll show you," he said, and promptly played a series of sultry, muffled sounds. I told him that it had sounded really cool, and asked if I could try playing the harp again. Derek nodded. I reached for his chrome-plated harmonica and wiped it clean. After taking a breath, I pressed it to my lips, and blew out several notes. This time the instrument emitted a series of high-pitched squeaks. Derek shook his head, and demonstrated his special technique by cupping his hands in front of it. I reached over, grabbed the harmonica from him, curved my fingers around it, and took a deep breath. This time I played a series of (non-honking!) notes.

"Not bad for a Yankee chick!" he exclaimed, and the two of us grinned at each other.

"Thanks for the lesson, Derek. Now I can add harmonica to some of the songs I've been writing."

"You've been writing songs, eh?"

I hadn't told many people about my song-writing at that point, but thought that Botticelli Boy might be someone who would appreciate it. And it seemed as though he did because, right before we entered the Green Park Tube Station, he flashed me a quirky smile and said, "Wait a minute, Luv! I want you to know that . . . well . . . since you've been 'ogging me 'arp, why don't you go ahead and keep it?" I clutched the harmonica between my breasts, and whooped with glee.

"Ohhh, thanks Derek!"

"Now 'ang on a minute," he replied.

"What?"

"I want you to know that I'm only parting with me 'arp because you're the first chick who's asked me for a lesson on it."

Chapter Seven

Diggin' Martin's Digs

I practiced my harmonica diligently and, by the time Janet and I knocked on the door of guitarist Martin Stone's communal Holland Park Avenue flat, I was able to play a passable rendition of the blues songs "Spoonful" and "Little Red Rooster." Although we did not recognize the tall, lanky guy who answered the door, he ushered us inside. Janet and I wandered down the hall, and peeked into the front parlor. It was sparsely furnished, with some bare mattresses lying on the floor. Then we walked towards a room at the back of the building, and discovered Martin sitting cross-legged on a rug. He was dressed in a flowing shirt, embroidered vest, velvet trousers, and beaded moccasins. Several of his flat mates were with him, passing around a couple of joints.

One fellow with wild red hair, named Moxie as it turned out, stood in a corner playing the flute. Although the room was smoke-filled, Feather Man spotted Janet and me through the haze. He rose, and embraced both of us in a welcoming hug. After the three of us had finally pulled apart, Martin invited Janet and me to hang out with him and his musician friends. We spent the afternoon chatting with Martin and his buddies, and listening to them jam. During that time, we learned that Savoy Brown's album, "Shake Down," was being released. At one point, I mustered up the courage to whip out my new harmonica, and play along during one of their lengthy jam sessions. It had been a wonderful day filled with meaningful moments, and esoteric conversation. By the end of our visit, Janet and I had been invited to crash at this communal flat for the remainder of the summer.

We took Martin and his buddies up on their generous offer, and checked out of Mrs. Zurita's Guest House in Clapham Common. Even though Feather Man's flat was basically unfurnished, Janet and I felt right at home living there. We were also pleased that it was located near Holland Park and Notting Hill Gate. During our stay, there were times when as many as half a dozen blokes would be crashing at this communal flat. Luckily, there seemed to be an unspoken pact among the guys not to mess with Martin's "chicks," so Janet and I felt free to roam around the premises as we pleased. We soon become so immersed in our new life there, that we had lost touch with Derek.

The longer we stayed with Feather Man and his friends, the more our interest in the London tourist scene began to wane. Instead, Janet and I found ourselves hanging out with the Hippies in Notting Hill Gate. We also took relaxing strolls through Holland Park, and attended various local gigs. By mid-July, Pink Floyd's "See Emily

Play" had reached number six on the UK charts, and the rock band Traffic released their hit single, "Paper Sun." Janet and I had been having a blast, and it felt as though the weeks were flying by. All of a sudden it was August—and time for us to return to the States.

On the morning we were scheduled to depart, our footsteps dragged as Martin walked the two of us to the vestibule. No one made a move to open the front door. "Why can't you chicks just stay here in London?" Feather Man was asking. I felt choked up, and unable to reply. Janet was brushing away the tears from her eyes.

"Oh, please don't make it any harder for us to go," she cried. I nodded as a fresh bout of tears began rolling down my cheeks. Feather Man was wiping his eyes, too, and the three of us exchanged another round of lingering hugs. Finally, one of us opened the front door, and Janet and I reluctantly waved good-bye to our beloved friend, Martin Stone. As we headed up the stairs towards the street, my feet felt like lead weights. Every step that we took was taking us further away from London—the city that felt like home.

When Janet and I boarded the TWA jet in Paris bound for New York, I longed to rush back into the terminal and book a flight that was heading to London. We knew that bands like the Nice had recently been formed, and Fleetwood Mac was about to make its debut at the Windsor Jazz and Blues Festival.

We would miss it all.

Once we were seated on the plane, I looked out the window at the billowy clouds. Visions of Feather Man and his friends flashed across my mind, and I swiped away several more tears. I glanced over at Janet and saw that her eyes were red-rimmed, as well. "I sure am going to miss London and all of our friends, aren't you?" she reflected.

"Yeah . . . I'm already homesick for Holland Park—and our flight hasn't even taken off yet!" The two of us were silent for several minutes, each of us lost in our own thoughts. Suddenly Janet turned towards me. She had a serious expression on her face, and I wondered what was up with my friend.

"You know, Kath, I've been thinking," she blurted out. "Why don't we go back to London?" Her words piqued my interest, and my eyes opened wide.

"You mean next summer?" Janet shook her head and explained that she wasn't talking about some corny tourist scenario. Instead, she was suggesting that we return to London for good. I nodded my head, and told her that renting a flat there would be a *dream-come-true*.

"Well then, why don't we move back there on . . . um . . . next February third, or something like that . . . ?" Janet replied as our plane began taxiing down the runway.

I reached over, squeezed her hand—and the deal was sealed.

Chapter Eight

Mighty Baby

After Janet and I returned to New York, we each secured part-time jobs and finished out the fall semester at college. In-between classes, we hung out on campus, and reminisced about our summer trip. There were times when we overheard our classmates bragging about their vacations, and all the tourist-y-things they'd done. Janet and I had gone sightseeing, as well, but we'd also made new friends and *lived* our experiences in London—even if it had been only for a summer.

Since that time, something had changed profoundly in me. I was determined to get back to London and live right in the middle of all the exciting music, fashion, and art that was being created there. Janet felt the same, and we vowed to save up cash from our jobs, take an official leave of absence from college, and rent a flat of our own in London. The hardest thing was telling our parents. When they heard the news, they were stunned, to say the least. Although

Janet and I felt guilty about disappointing them, it was *our* lives . . . and we knew what we wanted, without a doubt. So, the two of us booked an inexpensive charter flight that departed for Great Britain on (exactly!) February 3, 1968.

Once back in London, we located the nearest phone booth kiosk, and squished ourselves into it (with our luggage spilling out the door). Janet took her address book out of her bag and rang Feather Man's number. The guy who answered told her that Martin was now living in a communal house with his new band in Chelsea. Janet wrote down the particulars, and we dashed off towards the Chelsea Embankment, in sweet anticipation of our long-awaited reunion with the guitarist. When my friend and I entered Martin's digs less than an hour later, he laid his guitar down and jumped up from where he'd been sitting on the rug. "Ohh, it's Janet and Kathy come back to London," he exclaimed right before he enveloped the two of us in an effusive hug. Next, we all sat down together, and Martin told us that he had left Savoy Brown and was sharing this communal house with his current bandmates, drummer Roger Powell, rhythm guitarist Alan "Bam" King, and bassist Mick ("Ace") Evans. They had all been former members of the Action, a band formed by vocalist Reggie King. But a new group had subsequently emerged, which they named Mighty Baby.

During our reunion, Feather Man introduced us to his bandmates. Later that day, musician Victor Brox, a vocalist who also played organ and cornet with the Aynsley Dunbar Retaliation, stopped by. Victor had bought a house around the corner on Lots Road, and was looking to rent his two basement bedsits. Janet and I knew that bedsits were similar to studio apartments in the States, and we grinned at each other. "Well, it just so happens that Kathy and I are looking for a place to rent!" Janet informed Victor. The organist motioned for the two of us to follow him out the door and, soon, we were on our way to check out his rental bedsits.

As we rounded the corner onto Lots Road, Victor explained that he and his wife Annette, and their two daughters, lived on the main floor of his residence. After passing several row houses, Victor escorted us down to the basement level of his home. The front door had no lock and, when he pushed it open, a musty odor greeted our nostrils. The main area was practically empty, except for a pile of rubbish laying on the floor nearby. I kept glancing around, hoping to discover a kitchen that I had somehow missed. No such luck.

"So . . . ah . . . where's the kitchen?" I asked. Victor glanced down at the floor for several seconds before he replied.

"Sorry girls, but there's no kitchen facilities . . . yet." As he spoke, Janet wrinkled her nose behind his back.

"What? No kitchen?" she whispered in my ear. "Is this the Dark Ages, or something?" In the meantime, Victor was pushing open the first door on the left, which led to the largest of the two basement bedsits. Once we stepped inside, I saw that there were two twin mattresses laying on the floor. A wooden wardrobe had been positioned against the opposite wall, and two orange crates were serving as a pair of nightstands. A narrow window let in a thin ray of light from the street above, revealing a fine layer of dust on the floor, and walls that needed several coats of paint.

"Oh! And I forgot to mentioned that the loo's out back," Victor was saying. My eyes opened wide with shock. Janet and I followed him out of the bedsit towards the back of the basement. On the way, we passed by Victor's second bedsit that was to let. I peeked in, and discovered that it was miniscule in size. It was lacking a window, as well, which gave the room a rather dreary ambiance.

Janet and I hurried to catch up with Victor, who had already opened the door that led out to the yard. A blast of frigid wind hit us full force as the three of us exited the premises and made our way through the weeds that were laying in gnarly clumps throughout the area. Soon, we found ourselves face-to-face with a dilapidated outhouse, a sort of horror-movie version of the Leaning Tower of Pisa. This lean-to-loo was surrounded by various overgrown shrubs. Several broken bricks nearby indicated that there had once been an actual walkway leading to the outhouse. The three of us had no wish to linger around the loo, and we made a bee-line back towards the basement.

Once we were inside, it was obvious that the "tour" was over. It was also clear that Victor's lower level lacked even the most basic of amenities. I glanced at Janet and could tell by the frown on her face that she was grappling with this unsettling turn of events, as well. I told Victor that I wanted to confer privately with her in the front bedsit for several minutes. He nodded, and hung out in the main area, while my roommate and I entered the bedsit and closed the door behind us. Obviously, we needed to find an inexpensive place to live as soon as possible. But were we willing to put up with living in a place that had no kitchen, tub, or locks on the doors?

As my friend and I continued to wrestle with our emotions, I found myself trying to stifle the hysterical laughter that threatened to erupt from my belly. "Not exactly what we were expecting to find, is it, Kath?" my friend wryly observed. I nodded, and suggested that we take a final look around the place.

This time, Janet and I looked *inside* the wooden wardrobe, and checked out the firmness of the twin mattresses, too. At first glance, the orange-crate nightstands had looked to be rather primitive. Yet, upon further inspection, they took on a more rustic, farmhouse appeal—and would come in handy, as well. By far, the best feature of this basement bedsit was its window, which would allow some sunlight to filter in from the street above—once the pane had been cleaned.

Despite the fact that Victor's basement bedsits were far from renovated and we'd have to bathe at the Chelsey Baths, Janet and I knew that its close proximity to Mighty Baby's communal house made it an ideal location for us. I glanced around the room a final time and muttered, "Well, I guess this could be made into a cozy little place." Janet agreed and, when Victor entered the room less than a minute later, she asked him how much he would be charging for the weekly rent. When he told us that it was a mere, "Two pounds ten" she looked at me and grinned.

"Wanna take it, Kath?" she asked. I nodded, and we began digging through our purses for money to split the rental fee. Victor waited patiently as we counted our coins.

"Right then, girls! It's all settled!" our new landlord announced. He took the money from our hands, and shoved it into one of his trouser pockets. After scribbling a receipt for the rent, Victor told us that he would clear away the trash, put deadbolts on the doors, and that he was planning to install a kitchen in the basement level, as well. Janet and I watched as the bluesman stepped into the main room, and headed for the front door. "Cheerio, girls! I've got a gig coming up," he explained.

"Hey, Victor!" I called out after him. He turned back around.

"What is it, Luv?"

"Well, Janet and I aren't groupies or anything . . . but I was wondering if there are any other musicians besides you and Mighty Baby who live around here." Victor nodded his head, and told us that there was another rock group sharing a house a couple of doors down.

"Looks like this street's one big, happy family," Janet observed. The organist began to chuckle, and informed us that the band's name was, in fact, "Family." He swiveled around, and hurried out the door. Seconds later, we heard the clink of the iron gate at the top of the steps as it closed behind him. Janet and I wandered back inside our new bedsit abode, and marveled at our luck in securing a place to live in Chelsea, which was an artsy, super-hip area of London. It was a well-known fact that many musicians lived there, that Mick Jagger and Brian Jones had once shared a flat in nearby Edith Grove. There were also trendy boutiques situated along the Kings Road, such as the iconic Granny Takes a Trip. An antique market, a record store with listening booths, and the Chelsea Drug Store (a local landmark that was later immortalized in the Rolling Stones song "Sympathy for the Devil") were located there as well.

I walked over to the window of our new Lots Road basement bedsit, wiped a circle with my finger on the grimy pane, and peered out.

"Is this rock 'n' roll paradise, or what?" I gushed.

Chapter Nine

Lots Road

Before we moved into our new basement bedsit at 46 Lots Road, Janet and I wanted to glam it up a bit. So, we decided to apply several coats of Day-Glo interior paint on the walls. During this time, we stayed with one of Martin's friends who went by the name "Mouse." He had longish, dark hair, wide-set eyes, and a huge smile. His lanky frame had angular limbs that seemed to be in perpetual motion. Mouse lived with his sister and mother (a founder of the London Free School) in a house on Tavistock Crescent. We also learned that he was a roadie for the group Soft Machine that had been house band at the UFO Club, along with Pink Floyd.

Even though it seemed to be taking an inordinate amount of time to spruce up our basement bedsit, I was thrilled to be back in London, and wrote my brother, Alan, a letter.

Dear Alan,

As I write this letter, I'm hanging out with my friends from Mighty Baby at their house. We're listening to Peter Green's groovy guitar instrumental, "The Supernatural." It's from John Mayall's "Hard Road" album and I think you would really dig it! I have become immersed in the music scene here in London, and go to this blues club most every Sunday. It's called Studio 51 Ken Colyer Club, and lots of musicians, such as Eric Clapton, John Mayall, Tony McPhee, Duster Bennett, and Jo Ann Kelly jam there. I take my blues harp with me, and secretly jam with them at the back of the club. It's great practice, and an amazing opportunity to "play" with some of the best blues musicians on the planet. Oh, by the way, in less than two weeks Janet and I will be moving into a studio apartment that is located on the same block as the band Mighty Baby. We will also be living next door to an "underground" rock 'n' roll group called Family. Since we are moving into a house that is owned by a musician, we will have unlimited access to all sorts of instruments and records!

Love, Sister-Pie

Once the final coat of interior paint on the walls of our basement bedsit had dried, we moved in on a cold, blustery day. In reality, the two of us did not have many possessions to unpack; our meager belongings consisted of a Guild guitar, a trunk full of clothing, my backpack, several duffel bags, a collection of record albums (minus the phonograph!) and a giant poster of Grateful Dead guitarist, Bob Weir. Janet propped her guitar up against the wardrobe, and we were home! It was going to be rough living, this basement bedsit with its outhouse toilet and no kitchen or tub, but we reminded ourselves, again and again, that it was all worth it—just to be living in London.

In the weeks that followed, Janet and I continued to spend time hanging out with our musician friends at Mighty Baby's house. It was there that we read copies of the music publication *Melody Maker*, and listened to records by Cream, Procol Harum, Country Joe and the Fish, and Buffalo Springfield. When Martin announced one evening that members of Mighty Baby were planning to attend a gig by the progressive rock band Family at London's Middle Earth Club, Janet and I tagged along, eager to check out their sound.

Middle Earth was located in the Covent Garden area of London, and numerous hippies had already converged there by the time Mighty Baby's van pulled up outside this popular venue. As our Lots Road contingent entered the premises, the scent of marijuana and incense filled our nostrils. The decibel level was so loud, I could feel the music reverberating through the walls. We followed the crowd that was surging towards the stage where the five-piece band Family, who lived near us, was rockin' the club. The group's singer, a tall, slender bloke, commanded the stage while belting out the lyrics. He had a wide vocal range from warbling to scream-singing. The band also had a terrific drummer, and a guy who was playing a double neck Gibson guitar. Family's bassist (who also played violin and cello) was one of the best I'd ever heard, and another bloke with longish dark hair and a mustache sang backup vocals in addition to playing harmonica and saxophone.

Although the members of Family were dressed in shiny white suits that were reminiscent of the band Cream, their innovative music was difficult to categorize. It ranged from highly melodic ballads to songs that packed a powerhouse of raunchy rock 'n' roll. Many of their numbers were filled with quirky rhythm changes, as well, and I found myself intrigued by the teasing interplay between the instruments.

No wonder Family was one of Britain's hottest underground rock bands!

Hot in more ways than one, I mused.

But Janet and I weren't groupies dreaming about sleeping with Family.

Instead, I dreamed about performing my songs—as their opening act.

"Maybe someday," I muttered to myself.

When Family finished their final number, they exited the stage to thunderous applause. Members of the audience began to stomp and chant for an encore and, soon, our neighbors reappeared and were revving up the crowd, once again. As the final notes of their encore faded away, they hustled towards the backstage area. Even after they had disappeared from view, I continued to bask in the after-glow of Family's mesmerizing performance. In the meantime, the house lights went on and I watched as the roadies began packing up the various instruments, amplifiers, and microphones. As they rounded up the gear, I was secretly itching to have a go on the guitarist's unique Gibson. Janet and I had been intrigued by Family's gig at Middle Earth, and wondered when we'd get the opportunity to meet them in person.

One morning my roommate and I had just finished getting dressed, and we were planning to run some errands. I was wearing a velvet mini skirt and embroidered blouse, while Janet was dressed in a cobalt blue midi dress. As the two of us emerged from our basement bedsit, we noticed a white vehicle pulling up in front of Family's house nearby. Suddenly, the van door slid open and out stepped a guy who I recognized as Family's vocalist. He glanced in our direction, grinned, and said, "Well, now! What do we have here?" Janet and I walked over to him, and he introduced himself as Roger. Family's bassist exited the vehicle next, and approached in our direction. Once he had arrived by our side, he brushed back his fair, wiry hair, and smiled at Janet and me. Roger gestured towards his bandmate and said, "This here's Ric."

"You chicks living in Victor's place, eh?" the bassist inquired. Janet and I nodded, and then introduced ourselves. We also told Roger and Ric how we had met guitarist Martin Stone the previous year in Copenhagen, and crashed at his flat later that summer. I explained that Janet and I had fallen in love with London, so we decided to move back. As I spoke, two other members of Family exited the van, and we were introduced to guitarist John "Charlie" Whitney, and the band's muscular drummer, Rob Townsend. After twirling the pair of drumsticks that he was holding, Rob nodded to Janet and me, and then he headed inside Family's communal house. I turned back to Roger, Ric, and Charlie, and smiled at the three of them.

"By the way, Janet and I saw your gig at Middle Earth—and we love your sound!"

"Yeah, and we dig that double-neck Gibson guitar of yours, too!" my flat mate chimed in. Family's guitarist studied her for a moment, as though he was curious about her remark. It seemed like he was about to say something, but Family's sax player had exited the van and was sidling up to Janet and me. He seemed quite shy, and Roger introduced him as Jim, who handled saxophone, harmonica, and also sang back-up vocals. Jim bowed to Janet and me, muttered something about being pleased to meet us—and then he disappeared into Family's house. This left Janet and me standing outside in a circle with our neighbors Roger, Ric, and Charlie. It was clear that all the introductions had been made. Yet I found myself wanting to prolong the encounter.

"So," I glibly asked, "Are you guys from Liverpool?"

Roger shook his head, and began to laugh. "Christ! Why do all you bloody Yanks assume every British rock band is from Liverpool?"

"Yeah! It's nothing personal, Luv," Ric interjected. "But we happen to be from Leicester, not Liverpool."

I knew exactly where Liverpool was located on the map (along with millions of other rock 'n' roll fanatics) but was embarrassed to admit that I didn't know Leicester from Leinster! It was obvious that I had made a (major!) blunder, and I felt like slinking away down Lots Road, all the way to Battersea Bridge.

Chapter Ten

All in the Family

fter Janet and I chatted with Roger, Ric, and Charlie for several more minutes, they invited us into their home for a "cuppa" tea. There was no question as to whether my roommate and I would accept their invitation, and we followed them into their communal house. As we stepped inside, Rob and Jim were nowhere to be seen. Roger explained to us that Family had just returned from a tour, and his bandmates had gone straight to bed to catch up on some sleep. I could tell that guitarist Charlie had been politely trying to stifle his yawns, as well. He apologized to Janet and me for being so tired, and promptly headed towards his room. Janet and I were grateful that Roger and Ric had opted to continue hanging out with us. So, we followed closely behind as they led us into Family's front parlor. I glanced around the spacious area. A bass guitar and amp had been set up in the room, which was filled with sunlight from a lovely bay window.

Once the four of us sat down on the rug, roadie Harvey brought us cups of tea that he had prepared. Even though these members of Family were road-weary, the conversation that followed was lively. There were lots of questions being asked—and a couple of jokes thrown into the mix, as well. At one point, Ric picked up the bass guitar, plugged it into the amplifier, and started playing the bass line from one of Family's songs. Roger began singing along, and I felt privileged to be privy to their impromptu jam session.

As Roger and Ric began rocking out on yet another number, we heard voices in the hallway. Roger stood up and exited the room. When he returned, he had two "dolly-birds" in-tow. "Here come the groupies!" I half-jokingly thought to myself as the blonde-haired young women hunkered down on either side of Ric. I inwardly chided myself for being so judgmental. After all, they might not be groupies. Ric promptly set his bass aside, and the focus shifted to the new arrivals. Roger introduced them to us as Glynis and Dot, and the four females promptly gave each other the once-over. As I glanced at the two of them, I couldn't help but notice that their painted eyelashes looked like imitations of supermodel Twiggy. Dot had waist-length, platinum colored hair (that looked suspiciously like a wig), while her companion sported shoulder-length tresses of a more natural hue. I watched as Dot leaned over and gave Ric a quickie-kiss on the mouth. As she did so, her micro skirt hiked up, exposing a flash of her undies. An awkward silence ensued, and then the young woman named Glynis asked Janet and me how long we were on holiday in London. Once she learned that we had moved back to London on a permanent basis, Glynis and

Dot invited us to drop by their flat on nearby Stadium Street for a visit.

It was obvious that the majority of friends that Janet and I had made in London thus far were male musicians. So, we were pleased to have the opportunity to hang out with a couple of chicks for a change. We took Glynis and Dot up on their offer and, soon a friendship developed between the four of us. During one of our visits to their flat, Glynis and Dot warned us that a groupie named Anne would soon be knocking on our door, bearing gifts in an attempt to bribe us into helping her meet members of both Family and Mighty Baby. Sure enough, a couple of days later, Anne arrived on our doorstep. She was carrying several shopping bags filled with clothing and some tins of food. Within minutes, she was begging Janet and me to sneak her into the bedroom of Mighty Baby's handsome bass player, Ace.

Chapter Eleven

Ric's Rock 'n' Roll Revelations

When Family had the occasional day or two off the road, Janet and I enjoyed hanging out with them at their communal residence, where we drank tea and listened to their informal jam sessions. During one of these visits, the Leicester Lads had just returned from a prolonged stint on the road, and their bassist Ric told us about the realities of a rocker's life. "Must admit," he confessed, while rubbing his bleary eyes, "life on the road's not all it's cracked up to be—especially when our gigs are booked so close together. By the time we get back to London, we're bloody exhausted."

"Yeah, it seems like this is the first break we've had in weeks," vocalist Roger interjected. Ric stretched his arms, and then explained that their life was mainly spent living out of their luggage, eating at transport cafés, and longing for some home-cooked meals. As he spoke, it was difficult to imagine members of this popular band stopping along the motorway at some greasy café for a bite to eat.

"You guys have just shattered the glamorous myth of a rocker's life on the road," I announced with a chuckle. Ric rubbed his eyes, once again.

"Just telling you like it is, Luv . . ." He picked up his bass and plugged it into the amp nearby. Although he was wiped, Ric's passion for his music was still in evidence as he began playing a series of jazzy riffs that were intricate, yet fast-paced. Suddenly, he paused, and grinned at Janet and me.

"But don't get me wrong, girls. I'm not saying that Family's shows aren't fucking fantastic . . . because they are—and that's what makes it all worth it in the end."

Chapter Twelve

Teaming Up Together

Janet and I enjoyed living near the Kings Road in Chelsea, where we'd go window shopping with Glynis and Dot, wander through the various art galleries, purchase fruit from the green grocers, and check out the latest releases at the local record shop. We also sipped tea at guitarist Syd Barrett's flat in nearby Earls Court Square, and continued to hang out at Family's house. Although Janet and I felt fortunate to be living in London, our monetary savings had begun to dwindle to an all-time low. Luckily, I was able to secure a job as a charlady for a wealthy family in Chelsea, while Janet worked various secretarial assignments for a temporary employment agency. The two of us still managed to hang out with our Lots Road buddies, and attended many of their local gigs. Members of Family and Mighty Baby also squired us to shows by Ten Years After, T. Rex, Alan Bown, and various other rock musicians who were touring the circuit.

One evening, Janet and I went with Martin and his mates to a gig by the group Chicken Shack. This band featured a female singer/keyboardist named Christine Perfect (who soon married bassist John McVie, and later became a member of Fleetwood Mac). Christine was one of the few females we had heard about in the British music scene who not only wrote songs, but played an instrument in addition to fronting as a vocalist. As I watched her perform, I felt inspired that she had made it past the microphone-on-the-broomstick stage and was actually *doing her thing* as a chick blues musician in Britain.

Not long after Chicken Shack's gig, I picked up Janet's Guild guitar, and decided to try out two new songs that I had been "writing" in my head. First, I began with an instrumental called "Essence," and then I set the lyric sheet for my other song "Country Air" down on the bed next to me. After I ran through both numbers several times, Janet arrived home. I stopped playing, laid the Guild down, and said, "I hope it's okay that I borrowed your guitar, Jan." My flat mate set her bag on the nightstand, and sat down on her bed.

"No problem," she answered. "You can use it anytime."

"Oh, thanks! I've been working on a couple of *new* songs in my head, and wanted to try them out on your Guild." I went on to explain that my father had taught me various chords on his guitar, and that I'd taken classical piano lessons too. I even mentioned about my family's informal "orchestral" sessions where we'd sing Woodie Guthrie, Carter Family, and Leadbelly songs. During those fun-filled occasions, the four of us would sing harmonies together while I played the piano, my dad strummed his guitar, Alan fiddled away on his violin, and my mother played ukulele and kazoo.

Janet smiled, and said that she had studied both piano and guitar, as well. My roommate went on to tell me that she had started writing songs at an early age, had plenty of experience performing, and was still writing songs.

"Wow! What an amazing coincidence!" I gasped. I described how I'd been writing songs since I was eleven, and had performed with a modern dance company around that same time. Later, I attended the School of Performing Arts in New York City.

"It seems like we've had similar experiences when it comes to music, Kath!" The two of us kept smiling at one another, and I found myself confiding in Janet about the various songwriters and musicians that inspired me. "I really dig the lyrics in Donovan's song 'To Try for the Sun' because they help me believe in myself. You know what I mean . . . ?" Janet began to chuckle.

"Of course, I do!" she replied. "And the Lovin' Spoonful Song 'Do You Believe in Magic?' is an inspiring one, too," my friend added. Janet stood up and walked over to my bed. She sat down next to me, curious about the new songs I had been writing. So, I picked up her guitar, once again, and began playing "Country Air."

Janet scanned the lyric sheet that I had written, and began humming along. Soon, she was belting out the lyrics like a pro! In fact, her voice packed such a powerful punch, that I stopped singing altogether, and stared at her in awe. "Hey, where'd you get those *powerful pipes* of yours?" I gushed.

"It just comes naturally, I guess," Janet chortled. As I continued to stare at her, my mind was racing at breakneck speed.

What if . . .

What if . . .

"Listen, Janet! It's obvious that YOU should be singing the lead. So, why don't I handle the harmony, instead?" The two of us grinned at each other . . . And then we were singing *our* new song together.

Chapter Thirteen

The New Neighbor

Around that same time, our landlord Victor rented out the bed-sit next to ours to a keyboardist named Tony Kaye. Our new neighbor had shoulder-length hair, and he wore platform snakeskin boots along with his skintight trousers. Janet and I were pleased to have someone close by with whom to discuss our favorite bands, and gripe about the lack of amenities in Victor's basement level.

One afternoon shortly after Tony had moved in, he stopped by our bedsit. "Hello, girls! I'm on my way to the shops, and wondered if you need anything from there," he announced.

"Um, let's see now . . ." Janet replied with a chuckle. "We could use a tin of chocolate biscuits and a kitchen sink." Once our laughter had trailed off, we jotted down a couple of small grocery items, and gave him some money. After thanking Tony for his offer, Janet said that we had heard he was a musician, and were wondering what band he was gigging with. Our neighbor glanced down at the floor, and told us that he was currently between bands. I wanted to break the awkward silence that followed, so I asked whether it had been a portable organ that he had moved into his bedsit the other day.

"It just so happens that it was . . . but most chicks are more interested in my *other* organ," he wisecracked.

"Yech! Don't tell me you're one of those guys who automatically assume that Janet and I are groupies because we're chicks who hang out with the bands." Tony chuckled, and said that the thought had occurred to him.

"Well, now that we've cleared up that major misconception, it should be a load off your mind," I teased.

"It may be a load off the mind, but not me bod, Luv," Tony replied with a wink. He swiveled around, and promptly exited the room. We could hear his laughter echoing through the basement as he headed towards the front door.

Later that week, when Janet and I were rehearsing our two-part harmony for "Country Air," Tony reappeared in the doorway of our bedsit. I set the guitar down as our neighbor stepped into the room. "I hope you don't mind, but I couldn't help overhearing your music." He went on to tell us that the song sounded upbeat, and our harmonies blended well together.

"Ohh! Thanks!" Janet and I chorused.

"Have you thought about forming a chick rock duo?" Tony wanted to know. We nodded. His timely words of encouragement seemed to confirm that it was, indeed, possible for us to achieve our dream of becoming a trailblazing chick rock duo in Britain. It was a heady notion, and a ripple of excitement coursed through my body. Tony's words must have inspired Janet, as well, because a grin was stretching across her face. In the meantime, the keyboardist explained that he had only stopped by for a moment, because he had to split for an audition. We thanked him again for his support, and wished him luck. As he headed for the door, Tony called out over his shoulder, "Now remember to keep working on your music, girls, because it sounded very professional."

As soon as he had exited the house, I turned towards my flatmate and let out a whoop of glee. "WOW! Did you hear what he said, Janet?"

"Of course, I did! I was sitting right next to you!" my roommate chided me. She reached over, picked up her guitar, and began to play. At first, I thought Janet was just "having a go" on the instrument, but it soon became clear that she had started composing our fledgling female rock duo's *third* original number.

Chapter Fourteen

Impromptu Debut

Word soon spread through the Lots Road grapevine about the formation of our chick rock duo. When members of the band Family heard the news, they requested that Janet and I play some of our songs for them the following day. By then, we had written several new ones, and the two of us were excited to have this opportunity to share these original numbers with our Lots Road buddies. When Janet and I arrived at their house, we were greeted by members of Family. Musician/producer Dave Mason was present, too. Family was letting us use two of their electric guitars for our impromptu debut, and I had brought along an assortment of Hohner harmonicas.

While Janet and I checked the tuning of the guitars, I felt a mixture of nervousness and excitement, knowing that members of Family and Dave Mason were waiting in anticipation of our fledgling duo's performance to start. Once we were ready, we began with our two-guitar instrumental "Essence." It filled Family's front parlor with a melodic, yet powerful sound. Next, my friend and I launched into a song we'd written that showcased our two-part harmonies. Janet sang the lead with confidence, while I supplied a high harmony, and a bluesy harmonica solo. The more we played, everyone leaned closer towards us, grooving on our music.

Once the final notes of our mini-set had faded away, we glanced at our musician buddies, and saw that they were grinning at us. "That sounded cool, girls!" bassist Ric announced. Charlie nodded, and Roger suggested that, once we had enough songs for a set, Family would give our duo another listen.

"And maybe," he added, "You can come on tour as Family's opening act." I smiled at the renowned vocalist (who had the letters L-O-V-E tattooed on the fingers of his left hand) and felt a rush of gratitude that this British rocker was taking our music so seriously. Other band members chimed in, as well, suggesting that Janet and I meet with their manager, Tony Gourvish. We thanked them for inviting our duo to "audition" for them, and the exciting possibility of touring with Family.

My friend and I stood up, and I slipped my harmonicas in my jacket pockets. We were about to head for the door when Dave Mason suddenly called out to the two of us. "So,'" he asked, "What's the name of your band?" Janet and I had not yet decided on a name for our duo, and we were silent for a moment. Then I confessed that we had come up with a couple of names, but none of them had seemed quite right.

"Don't worry, Luv . . ." Roger replied.

"Yeah, we'll think of a good one for you," Ric chimed in.

I thought I heard a couple of snickers as we stepped into the foyer and headed down the front steps. I'd felt a momentary frisson of alarm, but was so enamored with the notion of touring the rock circuit with Family, that I managed to squelch it down.

In the meantime, Janet and I borrowed a couple of electric guitars from our other musician buddies, and embarked on a fresh round of songwriting and rehearsals. As the "buzz" about our new female rock duo continued to spread throughout Chelsea, the friendship we shared with our male musician friends deepened and evolved. Most importantly of all, these guys seemed to be thinking about the two of us more and more as fellow artists. They also began requesting that we critique the songs they were writing, and would often seek out our "professional" opinion regarding their various performances, as well.

Early one afternoon, when Janet and I had dropped by Family's home, their manager, Tony Gourvish ("Lotus," as we came to call him) arrived. As Ric introduced him to us, I noticed Tony's straight, dark hair and the quirky gap between his two front teeth. He was also sporting an interesting musician/businessman look, which included cool shades and traditional-style suit jacket. Tony shook our hands quite formally. "I've heard good things about your music," he told us. "But I've only popped 'round for a minute. When you chicks have enough songs for a set, we can discuss you going on tour as the opening act for Family." Despite Ric's cautionary advice about a rocker's hard life on the road, Janet and I were thrilled, and we thanked Tony for this amazing opportunity. Family's manager brushed a speck of lint off his suit jacket, and nodded at the two of us. "Right then! I need to split now, girls," he added. "And be sure to have enough songs to fill a set the next time I see you." We watched as Family's manager headed for the door, and then Janet and I sat down on the rug.

"Looks like Tony's on board with you opening shows for us," Roger announced, and we told him that it would, indeed, be a dream-come-true! Charlie leaned towards the two of us and asked whether we had finally come up with a name for our duo. I shook my head and explained that we were still grappling with it.

"You've got to get creative, that's what," he insisted.

"Yeah, something like . . . um . . . 'Emily Muff' would be cool, wouldn't it?" Ric suggested. His bandmates cheered, and Charlie said that the name had a nice ring to it. Janet and I nodded in agreement.

"Well, that's settled then." Roger declared. "Emily Muff's your new, official name." Ric cleared his throat.

"Listen up, everybody!" he announced. "From now on Janet will be called 'Em,' and Kathy, 'Moo.'" He glanced at his buddies, and grinned.

"Right, Lads?"

Chapter Fifteen

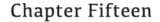

Yes Man

One rainy day not long after our neighbor Tony Kaye had gone to his audition, Janet and I heard someone knocking on the front door of Victor's basement level. I rushed to open it, and saw a young man standing on the stoop. He was dressed from head to toe in a deep shade of Kelly green, and holding a matching umbrella. As he brushed away the raindrops that were clinging to his blondish hair, he announced in a rather starchy tone of voice, "I'm Chris. Is Tony home?" He didn't wait for my reply. Instead, he pushed past me with what I referred to as a "You must be a groupie" glare. The stranger hustled towards Tony's bedsit, and our neighbor ushered him into the room.

Why did so many guys treat females as though they were expendable, non-entities? I wondered as I continued to loiter outside my bedsit. No doubt this cat named Chris had assumed that I was Tony's bimbo-bedmate. "Ugh! I can't wait to go on tour and knock the socks off guys who act like there's no place for chick musicians in the rock music scene," I huffed. When I entered our bedsit, Janet glanced up at me from where she was sitting on her bed. "What's all the commotion about, Moo?" she asked. I explained that it looked like Tony may have found himself a band, because some bloke named Chris had showed up, asking for him.

"You should have seen him, Em! He was all decked out in green, had a rock star vibe, and pushed past me as though I was Tony's groupie chick." As I spoke, we heard the front door open, and then the clank of the iron gate closing at the top of the steps. "How many seconds should we give Tony?' I asked.

"Ten at the most!" Janet replied with a grin. In less than that, the keyboardist was knocking on our door, and then he dashed inside. It was clear that Tony could barely contain his excitement as he told us that he'd just been invited to join a band that Chris and several other musicians were forming.

"Ohhh! That's great news!" I cheered.

"So, what's the name of your new band?" Janet wanted to know.

"They're calling it Yes!" Tony replied. He went on to inform us that the lineup included Chris Squire on bass, vocalist Jon Anderson, guitarist Peter Banks, and drummer Bill Bruford. "And now I'm on keyboards with the band, as well!" Janet and I rushed over, and gave him a congratulatory hug. Once the hoopla had died down a bit, I grinned at our neighbor.

"Are you going to remember us when you're rich and famous?" The keyboardist nodded his head.

"You promise?" Janet chided him.

"Yes!" Tony replied with a grin.

Chapter Sixteen

The Byrds and Chick Rock

Tony Kaye began rehearsals with his new band Yes, while Em and I continued to write songs for our chick rock duo. We were thrilled at the prospect of hitting the road with one of Britain's premier underground bands, and it seemed that the Leicester Lads were pleased for our duo, as well. Janet and I continued to attend their local concerts, and the gigs of other groups, too. One of the upcoming shows in London was by the Byrds, a well-known band that was on tour from the States. I was a fan of their music, and had seen them perform previously at Fordham University in New York. So, I was pleased when members of Mighty Baby and Family invited us to go with them to see this American band.

Middle Earth looked much the same as it had when Janet and I had first seen Family perform there. As our Lots Road contingent made its way inside the club, it was already jam-packed with patrons eagerly awaiting the start of the show. We joined the swarm of

Byrds fans who were surging towards the stage but, in the crush of the crowd, I quickly became separated from Janet and our other friends. I had no choice but to wait and find her after the show.

When Roger McGuinn dashed onstage with the rest of the Byrds several minutes later, they were bathed in a colorful array of lights. The band soon launched into its music, which seemed to be a more countryfied version of Roger's usual jangly Rickenbacker guitar. As they played selections from their upcoming album, "Sweetheart of the Rodeo," I recognized front man Roger McGuinn and bassist Chris Hillman, but there were two other musicians in the group who I wasn't familiar with. One of them, (who turned out to be Gram Parsons) was dressed in a flashy, embroidered suit, while the drummer was playing a driving beat in his Western-style shirt, boots, and blue jeans.

The Byrds was well-received by the audience. After members of the band had wrapped up their final encore, they headed towards the backstage area. Soon, the house lights went on, the roadies began packing up their gear, and the crowd slowly began to disperse. I was just about to begin my search for Janet when someone whispered a sultry "Hi there!" near my ear. I whirled around, and saw that it was the drummer for the Byrds who had been murmuring sweet nothings in my ear. He smiled, said that I looked very pretty, and introduced himself as Kevin. Then he asked me for my phone number. Although it was flattering to be singled out by him, it seemed as though the drummer might have mistaken me for some sort of groupie. When I hesitated to reply, he began describing how he'd joined the Byrds for its current tour, and that bassist Chris Hillman was his cousin.

Although Kevin seemed like a nice guy, I continued to wrestle with my thoughts. It was obvious that he wanted my phone number . . . but what else was he expecting? Finally, I reasoned that I couldn't possibly be considered a groupie, since I was a chick rocker who'd be going on a date with a fellow musician. "Actually, this is my landlord's phone number, but you can still reach me there," I explained as I scribbled down my information on a piece of scrap paper. Kevin tucked it in his jacket pocket, and said that he'd give me a call.

As I watched him make his way towards the backstage area, another wave of mixed emotions washed over me. Kevin was an attractive guy, yet I didn't want him to think of me as just another "Sweetheart of the Rodeo." After all, I hadn't exactly been standing in the audience with a Fender Telecaster guitar slung across my shoulder. So how the heck was he supposed to know that I was a rocker chick? I continued to grapple with my thoughts when Janet's familiar voice broke through my reverie. "Hey! Where have you been hiding?" she asked. "When I couldn't find you, I thought you had run off with one of the Byrds!" my friend added with a chuckle. As she spoke, I felt a blush spread across my cheeks, but kept silent. Luckily, Janet didn't seem to notice, and I followed her towards the exit.

Once the two of us met up with members of Family and Mighty Baby outside the club, they informed Em and me that they had picked up several groupies, and there was no longer room for us in the van. Upon hearing the news, Janet and I were pissed off with our so-called Lots Road buddies, but our protests went unheeded. Finally, we began searching for a taxi to take us home. "Dammit!"

I huffed. "Was the van so friggin' full that they had to give up our seats to a couple of groupies?"

"Guess they didn't want us to witness their sexual antics on the way back to Lots Road," Janet mused. An empty taxi pulled up to the curb near us, and we climbed inside. As it headed toward the Chelsea Embankment, I heard my friend mutter something about being glad that the two of us weren't a couple of air head star-fuckers. Her words reminded me of Kevin's request for my phone number.

"Listen, Em," I began. "Something happened back at Middle Earth." There was an awkward silence for a moment, and then I explained that the drummer for the Byrds had asked me for my number after the show. Janet's eyes opened wide.

"You're kidding, Moo! What did you say to him?"

By the time the cab pulled up in front of Victor's house, I had spilled the beans about my encounter with Kevin. I went on to explain that there had been no time for me to tell the drummer about our chick rock duo. However, I had finally given him my number—because I figured that we were two musicians going on a date.

Kevin telephoned me the following day, and I met him for lunch at a pizzeria near the hotel where members of the Byrds were staying. During the meal, I made sure to tell him about my rock duo, Emily Muff. I had thought that we would talk about it some more, but Kevin seemed reluctant to discuss it any further. I was puzzled, and wondered whether I had explained myself well. Or was the concept of a chick rock duo so foreign to this cat that he had ended up tuning me out?

When the meal was over, the drummer invited me to accompany him to a gig his band was playing that evening at the Speakeasy Club. I was eager to hear the Byrds play another gig, and accepted his offer. However, I was determined to try telling him again about my female rock duo later at the Speak.

When I met up with Kevin later at the club, his band's soundcheck had already wrapped up, and he escorted me to a nearby table. It seemed like the perfect time to remind him about my rock duo, and I opened my mouth to speak. At that very instant, a clique of groupie chicks ran over to our table. At first, Kevin attempted to be polite to his fans, but they continued to fawn all over him. So, the two of us stood up, pushed back our chairs, and we ran towards the nearest door. Kevin flung it open, and then we slammed it shut behind us. He and I stood in silence for a minute or two, thinking that the groupies might follow. Luckily, it seemed as though they had given up the chase, and we breathed a sigh of relief. Kevin and I glanced around, and discovered that we were standing in the middle of a deserted courtyard outside the venue. He smiled at me, and then apologized that we'd been interrupted by the groupies inside the club. "It's just part of being a musician in a big-name band," he explained.

As if I'd never heard of such a thing.

Hardly.

"Listen, I've been trying to explain that I'm a musician, too," I told the drummer. "In fact, my friend Janet and I have formed a chick rock duo here in London." Kevin's eyebrows skyrocketed upwards, and he asked me whether we were backup singers. I shook my head, and told him that my bandmate and I wrote original songs. "Our lineup includes electric guitars, keyboards, and blues harmonica. We sing powerful harmonies, too—and our duo may go on tour with the band Family."

Kevin frowned, and said he thought that Family was a heavy-duty rock band. He then asked how they were going to mic my duo's acoustic guitars. I sighed, and went on to explain that my female rock duo played bar chords, and groovy riffs on electric guitars. Kevin continue to stare at me. Then he shook his head and asked how chicks could have a rock duo.

Chapter Seventeen

Smokin'
at the Speak

Kevin's words sliced through the air and felt like they slammed into my solar plexus. I was momentarily stunned—but not speechless. In fact, I had the perfect retort. But just at that moment, two young men ran into the courtyard where we were standing and pulled the door shut behind them. They glanced at Kevin and me, and then back at the portal. I watched as they swiveled around and eyeballed us again—as if we might be a couple of undercover narcs. Finally, they seemed to decide that the two of us were cool, and they promptly began rolling a joint.

"Have you got a light?" one of them asked us. Kevin fished in his leather jacket pocket for a book of hotel matches, while I scrutinized the new arrivals further. There was something very familiar . . .

Then, in a flash of recognition, I realized that it was Mick Jagger who had asked us for a light!

Had Kevin also realized that we were about to share a joint with the Glimmer Twins? I struggled to keep my cool as I sneaked another peek at these famous rock stars who were standing only a couple of feet away from us. Mick Jagger appeared a bit shorter than I had imagined he would be. Keith Richards had this groovy aura about him. At the same time, he seemed a bit more rugged-looking than when I had spoken with him at the Phone Booth Club over two years ago.

I glanced around again, my mind taking in the entire tableau:

Mick's piercing blue eyes and mega-watt smile . . . The breeze tousling Keith's hair . . . and the courtyard bathed in the rays of the oncoming sunset.

It was an unexpected, momentous occasion, and I hoped that I appeared somewhat nonchalant, yet also super-cool. That shouldn't be too difficult to do . . . right? After all, I had already met rockers Keith, Bill, and Brian—and other well-known musicians such as Dave Mason, Aynsley Dunbar, Victor Brox, and bluesman John Mayall. My bandmate and I had hung out with members of Family, Yes, Savoy Brown, and Mighty Baby, as well. So, what was the big deal about smoking a couple of joints with the Glimmer Twins?

The truth of the matter was it took every ounce of my self-control not to shriek, "Oh, it's Mick and Keith!"

Not to mention jumping up and down.

"Keep your cool, girl!" I silently chanted over and over like a soothing mantra in my mind. The rhythmic phrase calmed me down so I could relax, at least a little, by the time Keith passed me the joint. His fingers brushed mine as I took it from him. These were the same fingers that played powerful riffs on his Gibson guitar. I inhaled . . . and passed the reefer along to Kevin. While the drummer took several puffs, I turned back towards Keith. I was just about to remind him that we had met at the Phone Booth Club. But Mick opened his mouth first, and all eyes seemed to be on him as he spoke to Kevin. "Hey, Man! You're with the Byrds, aren't you?" The drummer nodded. Then Keith grinned, and said that he and Mick had always been fans of the Byrds. Mick Jagger took the joint from Kevin.

"Yeah, we're here tonight to check out your gig, man," Mick replied. At this, Kevin seemed to puff out his chest. The reefer was passed around the circle again. Soon, the male musicians began talking shop. I longed to whip out my Hohner harp and play Mick Jagger my latest rendition of "Little Red Rooster." So, I reached for it in my purse, but my harmonica wasn't there. Ugh! It was the *only* time I had forgotten to stash it in there before I left the house.

When the joint finally returned to Mick, he took a parting toke—and flicked the tiny roach over the courtyard wall. And with that, the Glimmer Twins disappeared back into the club. Kevin wiped his brow, while I leaned back against the courtyard wall. "Wow!" the drummer blurted out. "I knew there was a rumor going around that the Stones might show up at my gig tonight, but I didn't think they were actually going to make it!"

"Well, they sure showed up!" I quipped. Smokin' at the Speak with these world-famous rock stars had been exhilarating . . . and a bit overwhelming, too. It was obvious that the drummer and I were still reeling in disbelief (partly from the joint, partly from the mind-blowing circumstances).

Kevin glanced back at the courtyard door and smiled. "It's not every day you get to share a joint with Mick and Keith, is it?"

Chapter Eighteen

A Vision for the Future

Around this same time, Em and I decided that we'd had enough of putting up with the rigors of our Lots Road basement bedsit, where there was still no sign of any upgrades being made. So, we rented a spacious flat on Holland Road, complete with a kitchen, indoor toilet, two sinks, and tub. Not long afterwards, guitarist Martin Stone asked if he could move in with us, and we welcomed him into our home. After all, he had let us stay at *his* Holland Park Avenue flat during the Summer of Love, and he was one of our most cherished friends. We offered Feather Man the use of our front parlor, and soon his groovy guitar licks could be heard soaring throughout the flat.

My bandmate and I continued to rehearse, and Martin invited our female rock duo to make an informal appearance at one of Mighty Baby's gigs. We appreciated the opportunity to test the waters at this show, and Em and I were feeling fired up when we arrived at the venue.

It was the first time that our duo had been offered a gig in Britain, and it felt fantastic to be appearing before a live audience. Our performance went smoothly, and Emily Muff was well-received by the crowd. My bandmate and I were super-pleased, and felt that the experience had helped to prepare us for our future role as Family's opening act. Not long after our duo's performance at Mighty Baby's gig, I purchased a Yamaha flute which we promptly added to our lineup.

Although Em and I were still writing songs, I was now working in an office in the East End of London, and she had various secretarial temp assignments throughout the city. Despite our heavy schedule, we continued to take in the local music scene. Among the many performances that we looked forward to attending was the Incredible String Band at London's Royal Albert Hall. Although this group was considered by some to be a duo, its lineup also included Robin Williamson and Mike Heron's girlfriends, who not only performed with them, but had appeared on several of the String Band's albums, as well. Our Lots Road buddies had teased Em and me that we bore a striking physical resemblance to musicians Robin and Mike of the Incredible String Band. So, we headed to our local record store to see if the physical similarity was true.

Once the two of us perused the covers of the String Band's albums "The Hangman's Beautiful Daughter" and "Wee Tam and the Big Huge," there could be no denying the physical resemblance between Janet and me and musicians Robin Williamson and Mike Heron.

Still, there was a difference—and it wasn't just gender.

Even though these male multi-instrumentalists were talented musicians with a flair for intricate lilting melodies, their music was notably softer than the bar-chord approach that was fast becoming a hallmark of Emily Muff's repertoire. Many of the themes in the String Band's lyrics focused upon riddles, fairies and witches, while our music had a harder edge, laced with an occasional angst.

As the house lights dimmed in the Royal Albert Hall on the day of the Incredible String Band's concert, Janet and I watched as Robin appeared onstage and picked up his guitar. He was quickly followed by a dark-haired young man, Mike Heron. Both musicians took their places among an array of instruments. As they paused to adjust their microphone stands, Janet leaned towards me and whispered, "It's a bit like looking in the mirror, isn't it?" We listened then as Robin began singing in a lilting voice, his crystal-clear intonation breathtaking. Soon, Robin and Mike's brunette, long-haired girlfriends, Rose and Licorice, joined them onstage. Rose played bass, violin, recorder, percussion, and sang backup vocals. Robin's girlfriend, Licorice, also played percussion and organ while handling backup vocals.

Throughout the concert, the Incredible String Band's music had been inventive, and a change from the decibel-heavy performances we usually attended. Once the show was over, Em and I rose from our seats. We followed the crowd towards the nearest exit, but it was slow-going. Suddenly, my bandmate pointed upwards, towards the rows of seats in the topmost tiers. "Wow, Moo! Imagine our duo playing a concert here at the Royal Albert Hall!" As she spoke, I envisioned Emily Muff's songs soaring throughout this illustrious venue, and replied that it would, indeed, be a dream-come-true.

Chapter Nineteen

Joe Boyd

I had been intrigued by the Incredible String Band's concert at the Albert Hall, and was curious to meet this group in person. With that in mind, I went about setting up an appointment with their manager, Joe Boyd. I recalled seeing that this manager/producer and his company, Witchseason Productions, were listed on the String Band's albums. So, I phoned his office, and he agreed to meet with me. Joe Boyd was well-known in the London music scene. In addition to handling the Incredible String Band, he had also produced Pink Floyd's debut single, "Arnold Layne," and co-founded the UFO Club—where Derek had taken Janet and me the previous summer.

When I arrived at the office of Witchseason Productions on the day of my appointment, a tall, handsome man with longish brown hair greeted me in the hallway. He introduced himself as Joe Boyd, and invited me into his office. I took a seat, and told him that I appreciated the time he was taking out of his busy schedule to meet with me. Joe Boyd smiled warmly, leaned back in his chair, and I continued. "Actually, I'm here because I feel that my duo, Emily Muff, has a special connection with the Incredible String Band." The businessman appeared to be regarding me with renewed interest, and I went on to explain that my female rock duo had been invited to tour with the band Family as their opening act.

"Aha! So, *you're* with that new female duo I've been hearing about!" Joe Boyd replied. He smiled at me again, and asked about Emily Muff's line-up. I told him that my bandmate, Janet, and I wrote our own material and that we played electric guitars, keyboards, woodwinds, and blues harmonica. I went on to say that Janet was the lead singer, while I handled the vocal harmonies. Joe Boyd leaned forward in his chair, and indicated that he would keep an eye out for news of my duo in the local music scene. He also arranged for me to rendezvous with members of the Incredible String Band at their Leinster Towers Hotel the following day. At the conclusion of our meeting, Joe Boyd walked me to the door. We then shook hands, and he told me if my plans did not work out with Family, he might be interested in representing my female rock duo.

I met Mike and Rose the following day in the lobby of the Leinster Towers Hotel, where Robin and Licorice soon joined us. I told them how much I had enjoyed their concert at the Albert Hall, and also mentioned about my female rock duo. Robin seemed pleased that I was a fellow musician, and explained that the Incredible String Band was on its way to a recording session. It turned out that they were headed to the Kensington area. Once Robin heard that I lived on Holland Road, he offered to give me a lift in their van, so that we could hang out a bit longer. Along the way, both Robin and Mike plied me with questions about my chick rock duo, including the instruments that we played, and the style of our music. We continued to talk shop until the String Band's van pulled up at the corner of Earls Court Road and Kensington High Street.

As I opened the door and stepped onto the curb, Robin leaned towards me and said that his band would remain in London for several more days. He went on to suggest that I telephone his hotel the following day, so that Janet and I could meet with him before he returned to the String Band's residence in Brynbarian, Wales. When I arrived home after my meeting with the Incredible String Band, I saw that Janet was stretched out on her bed, reading Hermann Hesse's *Magister Ludi*. She set the book aside, and I gave her a recap of my meetings with Joe Boyd, and the Incredible String Band—including Robin's invitation to get together with him before he returned to Wales.

I phoned Robin at his hotel the next day, and gave him Emily Muff's address. He said that he had a busy schedule, but would try and stop by for a visit. Later that afternoon, he appeared on our doorstep. Our flat mate, Martin, happened to be out at the time, and Em and I invited Robin inside. We had a wonderful time chatting together and, during his visit, he described in detail about the String Band's cottage, "Tryhidd." Their home was located in Brynbarian, Wales, and it sounded like an idyllic country retreat with few distractions and plenty of time to write songs and rehearse. By the time Robin left our flat that day, he had invited Janet and me to visit him in Wales, and the three of us agreed to keep in touch.

Buoyed up by Robin's description of the String Band's home, Janet and I began discussing the pros and cons of renting a cottage in the countryside for Emily Muff. After all, it would give us time to write more songs and rehearse away from the hubbub of London. We knew that bands like the Rolling Stones and Traffic had various retreats where they wrote songs and rehearsed in privacy. Perhaps being able to have some peace and quiet without our long commutes and the distractions of city life was exactly what we needed. By the end of our discussion, Em and I had decided that it might, indeed, be a good idea for us to rent a cottage of our own fairly soon.

Chapter Twenty

Jimi, Marty, Grace, and Jim

Members of Family invited Em and me to accompany them to the Woburn Music festival, where they were booked on the same bill as the Jimi Hendrix Experience. Of course, we jumped at the chance to attend this event. After all, it was an amazing opportunity to witness this world-famous guitarist perform live with bassist Noel Redding and drummer Mitch Mitchell.

On the day of the festival, we managed to secure a stellar, front/center view so that we could lean up against the stage. After Family had rocked out with their impressive set, Em and I felt lucky to be present to witness the Jimi Hendrix Experience perform. The crowd greeted the trio with a roar of thunderous applause. Jimi was dressed in velvet trousers, sporty hat, and a colorful, flowing shirt. We watched as he prowled around the stage playing guitar solos that were off the charts. At other times he gnashed his instrument with his teeth—while stretching each note (and his trousers) to the limit. The setlist included "Foxy Lady," "Voodoo Child," and "Purple Haze." Jimi's hypnotic voice and stellar rhythm section were so tight, I thought my jaw would never close again! Watching this icon strutting his stuff just a few feet away from where Janet and I were standing seemed surreal, and I felt a feeling of loss as the final notes of the Jimi Hendrix Experience faded away.

In early September of 1968, two American bands, Jefferson Airplane and the Doors were booked to headline the show at London's Roundhouse in Chalk Farm. Em and I were excited to see these bands perform, and also looking forward to meeting up with our friend, Jeff Dexter, who was impresario/DJ of the show. When the two of us arrived outside the venue on the day of the event, the area was so jam-packed it was tough going as we attempted to make our way through the throng to the backstage entrance. Janet flexed her muscles in mock display and said, "I hate to be a pushy chick . . . but . . ." As we continued to navigate our way through the crowd, I suddenly felt someone tapping me on the shoulder. After motioning for my friend and me to stop, I turned around and saw that a dark-haired woman with blue eyes and a friendly smile had been trying to get my attention. She was accompanied by a handsome man with brown hair and high cheek-bones. I was just about to ask what was the matter . . . when it suddenly dawned on me that they were the Jefferson Airplane vocalists Grace Slick and Marty Balin! "Why are these rock stars roaming around outside the Roundhouse, when they were supposed to be backstage prepping for their gig," I wondered.

I tried to keep the shock of our impromptu rendezvous with these two megastars from registering on my face. But it was too late; my mouth and eyes had already widened in surprise. Janet seemed to have recognized these rockers, too, and smiled warmly at them. Marty and Grace explained that the Airplane had only just arrived in London. There had been no time for them to grab a meal before their Roundhouse gig, and they were hungry. Then Grace asked whether we could drive them somewhere to get a bite to eat before the show. As she spoke, I found myself wondering why their roadies weren't hovering around, making sure that members of Jefferson Airplane had plenty to eat, and that everything was running smoothly. Although Em and I didn't personally have a car, we assured Marty and Grace that we'd somehow find them a lift so they could get some grub. Janet volunteered to be in charge of this task, and I watched as my friend hurriedly disappeared into the crowd.

While the three of us awaited her return, I noticed that Grace kept glancing around. Was she feeling uptight that Jefferson Airplane fans might suddenly recognize the two of them, and go bananas? I was amazed that the fans standing less than a foot away from us had failed to recognize their idols stranded in the crowd. On second thought, however, Marty and Grace were so casually dressed, they looked more like concertgoers, rather than international rock stars who would soon be performing on the Roundhouse stage.

As Marty, Grace, and I continued to await Janet's return, I took the opportunity to let them know how much I grooved on Jefferson Airplane's West Coast sound. They seemed pleased, and I found myself telling them about Emily Muff. Both Jefferson Airplane vocalists seemed genuinely interested in our duo, and wished Janet and me luck on our rock 'n' roll journey. It was refreshing that

Marty and Grace had not been surprised to hear about two chicks rockin' out on electric guitars in the London music scene, and I appreciated their enthusiasm for Emily Muff.

Soon, Janet returned with news that she had found a ride for Marty and Grace. They thanked her for helping them out and, within minutes, these rock stars were on their way to the nearest eatery. I smiled at Em, and told her how much I appreciated the effort she had made to find them a lift, as well. "It's lucky that I spotted someone I knew who could give them a ride," she replied.

The two of us resumed making our way towards the backstage entrance, and I mentioned that I'd told Marty and Grace about our chick rock duo. I went on to say that they had seemed very supportive of Emily Muff, and had wished us luck on our rock 'n' roll journey. Upon hearing this, Janet seemed pleased that they were hip to our band, but said she wasn't surprised—since they lived in the San Francisco area, which was such an open-minded city. As we continued to make our way through the crowd, I confessed to Em that I wished that the Airplane's lead guitarist, Jorma, had also been stranded outside the Roundhouse, along with Marty and Grace.

"That way, I would have had the opportunity to tell him how much his instrumental 'Embryonic Journey' sends tingles up my spine."

Once my bandmate and I arrived at the backstage entrance, we made our way inside, and were able to rendezvous with our friend Jeff Dexter. I noticed that the DJ seemed a bit preoccupied. He began telling us that Marty and Grace had still not showed up, and asked if we had seen the two of them. Janet and I began to laugh, and proceeded to give Jeff a rundown on how we'd met them *outside* the Roundhouse venue. Next, Em recounted the saga of securing a lift so they could get some grub.

When members of Jefferson Airplane finally appeared onstage for their set, Grace and Marty, along with their bandmates Paul Kantner, Jorma Kaukonen, Jack Casady and Spencer Dryden performed an amazing set that wowed the Roundhouse crowd. It was obvious that the Airplane would be a hard act to follow.

I admired Jim Morrison's poetry and soul-searching lyrics, and cheered along with the crowd when the Doors first made their appearance at the Roundhouse gig. Keyboardist Ray Manzarek, drummer John Densmore, and guitarist Robby Krieger all played a stellar set, but it was a bit unsettling that Jim Morrison's vocal delivery seemed unusually dilute. By the time the band had launched into a lengthy rendition of their hallmark song, "End of the Night," it seemed as if the crowd's enthusiasm had cooled considerably—and I found myself hoping that it had merely been an off-night for this rock 'n' roll icon.

Chapter Twenty-One

DJ John Peel

In the meantime, Janet had secured an invitation for Emily Muff to meet with renowned BBC Radio 1 disc jockey John Peel at his office in London's Park Square Mews. When we arrived on the evening of our appointment, we were greeted by John Peel with a friendly smile after a brief wait at the door. Once introductions had been made, the sandy haired DJ led us to an area that appeared to be utilized as both personal and office space. He apologized for the delay in answering the door before picking up the phone receiver and resuming the conversation our knock must have interrupted. Taking the opportunity to glance around the room, my eyes grew wide when I saw the various stacks of demo tapes piled high towards the ceiling.

"Check out all those cassettes over there," I whispered in my bandmate's ear. She nodded, and muttered that she hoped Emily Muff's future demos wouldn't end up in one of John Peel's "slush piles." As the two of us continued to cruise around the room, the DJ wrapped up his telephone conversation. Once he noticed that we had been checking out the tapes, John Peel told us that he received numerous demos on a regular basis. He went on to explain that he tried to listen to as many of them as possible. While he was speaking, his telephone chimed again. After he had finished this conversation, the DJ apologized and said that it seemed as though his phone was constantly ringing off the hook.

Em and I reassured him that we understood he was very busy, and John Peel thanked us for our patience. He then asked about the status of Emily Muff, and we told him about our music, the duo's line-up, and a projected tour with the rock band Family. Janet and I also mentioned that we had been thinking about moving to South Wales for a while, so we would have uninterrupted time in which to write more songs and rehearse. Upon hearing this, John Peel indicated that he thought renting a country cottage seemed like a good idea. He also offered to give Emily Muff's music a listen when our duo returned to London.

"Kathy and I have been keeping an eye out for other chick rock duos on the scene, but we haven't heard about any other ones here in London," Janet remarked. The BBC Radio 1 disc jockey thought for a moment. He then announced that, as far as he knew, Emily Muff had the distinction of being the First Female Rock Duo in the history of British rock 'n' roll.

"It's super exciting that our band has that honor!" I exclaimed. Before John Peel had a chance to reply, his telephone was chiming again. He picked up the receiver, and asked if he could ring them back. It was obvious by the number of calls the DJ was receiving that we needed to wrap up our visit, so I slipped on my jacket. John Peel walked us to the door and apologized, yet again, for all of the interruptions during our visit. "That's OK," I replied. "It was a pleasure to meet you!"

"Yeah, thanks so much!" Janet concurred. The DJ smiled, shook our hands, and said that he had enjoyed meeting us, as well. Despite the brevity of our visit, Em and I were pleased that this iconic BBC Radio 1 DJ had shown an interest in our music—and that he had confirmed that Emily Muff was, indeed, the First Female Rock Duo in Britain.

Chapter Twenty-Two

A Rehearsal Retreat

After our meeting with DJ John Peel, I continued to chat with Em while we searched for a taxi to take us home. "It's so cool that he confirmed Emily Muff's status as the First Female Rock Duo in Britain!" I remarked. Janet nodded, and said that she was also pleased that he had encouraged us to rent a cottage in the country. As we continued to search for a vacant cab, my bandmate mentioned that she'd been thinking about the Incredible String Band's home in Brynbarian, Wales. I confessed that Robin's description of Tryhidd kept echoing through my mind, as well. Finally, a vacant taxi came into view, and the two of us flagged it down. After we made ourselves comfortable inside the vehicle, my friend leaned forward towards the driver, and instructed him to take us to Euston train station. As the cab pulled away from the curb, I stared at her.

"Euston Station? Hey, wait a minute. Em! We haven't even packed!"

"Look, I know that going to Euston is a spur-of-the moment detour tonight, but there's no time like the present, eh?" Janet replied. My friend went on to explain that she thought newsstands there might sell periodicals with ads for residential rentals in Wales. When she finished speaking, I nodded, and began humming lyrics to the Emily Muff song "Country Air."

> *"The fog has swept the city,*
> *So thick you just can't see,*
> *It weighs you down with concrete,*
> *And just won't let you be,*
> *Come down to the country with me."*

Once we arrived at the terminal, it turned out that Em's hunch had been right; several newsstands there sold periodicals that featured classified ads for rental homes in South Wales. Soon, the two of us were sitting on a bench inside the station, flipping through the various advertisements as well as our newly purchased map of South Wales. With pen-in-hand, we began circling several ads that looked promising. There was one in particular that had sparked our interest. It had been posted by the Lacey family, who had a cottage for rent in the town of St. David's, in Pembrokeshire, South Wales. We decided to telephone them right away.

Em inserted the requisite coins in the pay phone. I stood nearby, ready to take any notes, if needed. She dialed the long-distance number and Mr. Lacey answered the phone. The two of them continued to chat for several minutes. By the smile on Janet's face, I could tell that they had a comfortable rapport. When she grabbed my arm and whispered, "Oh, I think this is the one!" I nodded my head in assent—and Em promptly booked the rental. After hanging up the phone, she explained that Mr. Lacey had mentioned that his family was friends with Swami Satchidananda in Ceylon. Once he heard that Janet and her college buddies had attended several kirtans hosted by this Swami, Mr. Lacey had offered to rent his cottage to us on the spot.

In preparation for Emily Muff's move to Wales, we gave notice to our Holland Road landlord, and our employers. We also broke the news to our flat mate, Martin. Feather Man told us that he understood why we were taking some time out to rehearse in Wales, and he moved back to the Lots Road area. Janet and I also informed Family's manager that we had rented a cottage in Wales for several months, in order to concentrate on Emily Muff. Upon hearing the news, Lotus assured us that he would welcome our duo back into the Family fold when we returned to London.

Chapter Twenty-Three

The Welsh Bard

Around the same time that Em and I booked our cottage in Wales, the rock group Cream had disbanded, the Who released their smash hit single, "Magic Bus," and John and Yoko had appeared as Two Virgins on their controversial album cover. No doubt about it, my friend and I were going to miss the London music scene. However, we both felt that it was important for us to sequester ourselves away for a while, in order to have uninterrupted time in which to write songs and rehearse. On the day of our departure, we traveled by train to Cardiff, Wales. From there we would transfer to a local train bound for Haverfordwest, and then a bus would take us the rest of the way to the coastal town of St. David's.

Although we both were carrying luggage and various instruments with us, Janet had also brought along a large, metal trunk. Once we arrived in Cardiff, it was difficult hauling it through the station while searching for the track where the Haverfordwest-bound train was to arrive. As we glanced around, I noticed a man watching us. The stranger had wispy brown hair, and he was holding a guitar case. He must have overheard Em and me discussing about the train to Haverfordwest, because he called out to us, asking whether we were traveling there. He seemed quite friendly, and we nodded. The stranger pointed to a platform that was across the railway station. "It'll be coming in over there," he said in a lilting Welsh accent.

Janet and I thanked him for this information, and he told us that he was traveling to Haverfordwest, as well. The Welshman helped us carry Janet's trunk to the platform he had indicated, and then introduced himself as Meic Stevens. We told him our names and, several minutes later, the three of us watched as the train bound for Haverfordwest approached the station. As it slid along next to the platform and then came to a stop, I peered inside the windows and saw that the carriages were filled with rows of austere, wooden benches. Once we had boarded the train, Meic motioned for Janet and me to have a seat. We nodded, and watched as he lifted Em's cumbersome trunk effortlessly onto one of the benches near the front of the carriage. He then took a seat next to us. Em thanked Meic for his help, and said that it had been a crazy idea to lug that "baby" all the way from London. The Welshman chuckled, set his guitar between his knees, and said that the trunk was, indeed, a bit on the bulky side. The three of us were silent for several minutes, and then Meic asked us how long we planned to stay in Haverford-west. When he learned that Janet and I had rented a cottage in St. David's, he told us that he lived on a farm in Solva, which was not far from where we would be staying.

"Maybe we can all get together sometime," he suggested. Considering how Janet and I had met guitarist Martin Stone the previous summer, it didn't seem so far-fetched that we had come across a musician in the Cardiff railway station who was suggesting that we meet again. Janet pointed to Meic's guitar case, and asked whether he was a musician. The Welshman nodded, and informed us that he was just returning home from his recording session in Cardiff. He paused for several seconds . . . and it seemed as though he was waiting to see whether we would recognize him as "The Welsh Dylan."

"I'm afraid that Janet and I aren't up on the music scene in this area of Great Britain," I confessed.

"Oh, that's quite all right, Luv," he replied with a grin. "I didn't expect you Yanks to have heard of me—yet!" Meic reached into his knapsack and pulled out an EP-45 of his latest songs on the Wren Record label. I examined the label more closely, and noticed that the names of the songs: "Can Walter," "Hwiangerdd Mihangel," "Glaw yn y Dail," and "Lan a Lawr," were in Welsh. He asked whether I would like to keep that record. I nodded my head, and he handed it to me. I thanked him for giving the EP to us, and carefully tucked it among my belongings. Our new Welsh friend then informed us that BBC Wales-TV had asked him to appear in a Meic Stevens special program that would air later in the year. He went on to tell us that a film crew was supposed to come to his farmhouse in Solva soon.

"Speaking of performances, would you play us a tune?" I requested. Meic nodded, snapped open the hinges of his case, and removed a well-worn acoustic guitar. While he began to tune the instrument, I glanced around the railway carriage and wondered whether any of the other (three!) passengers realized that they were about to be serenaded by a prominent Welsh folk singer. Then I leaned back against the wooden bench while Meic Stevens began to play a soulful ballad. Although the lyrics were foreign to me, his melodic chords and lovely voice created a soothing ambiance in the railway carriage. When the number came to an end, our new friend explained that many of his songs were based upon historical Welsh folk tales.

Em requested that he play us another tune, and "The Welsh Dylan" began singing a ballad called, "Glaw yn y Dail." Once the song was over, he tucked his guitar back into its case and asked, "So what have you ladies been up to in London?" I explained that Janet and I had formed a rock duo, and that we were moving to St. David's in order to have uninterrupted time to write songs and rehearse.

"So, you're musicians, then! What's the name of your group?"

"Emily Muff," I replied.

Meic's eyebrows arched upwards. "Emily Muff?" he exclaimed. Janet nodded, and told him that a rock band in London named Family had given us the name. I leaned forward, and said that they had also invited our duo to tour with them as their support band when we returned to London. Meic Stevens was silent for a moment while he continued to stare at us, and then he shook his head.

"That sounds like a great opportunity, girls . . . but . . . ah . . . are you sure that Emily Muff's the right name for your band?" Janet asked what was wrong with it, and I told him that we thought it had a catchy sound. "Well, it may have a catchy sound but . . . oh shit! Listen up girls!" he declared. "This is probably none of my business, but you both seem like a couple of nice chicks. Don't you know what the word 'muff' means?" Em and I replied that we had heard about musician Muff Winwood.

"I'm not talking about Steve Winwood's brother!" Meic Stevens huffed. "Oh, man! I can't believe you girls don't know that 'muff's' the slang word for cunt."

"Whaaat?" I gasped. "You must be joking!" The Welshman replied that the joke was apparently on us. Em and I continued to reel in disbelief.

"Of all the lowdown . . ." my bandmate growled. Meic continued to shake his head in disbelief, and told us that we must be the most naïve females on the planet. I glanced over at Janet and sighed.

"What'll we do now?" I asked her. "Do you think Family gave us that name as a practical joke, or something?" By that time, Janet's body had grown tense, as if she wanted to smash her fist through the nearest window.

"Aggh!' she groaned. "This means that every time Kathy and I go onstage to play a gig, we'll be known as Emily's cunt."

Meic Stevens continued to stare at the two of us.

"So, which one of you is Muff?" he asked.

Chapter Twenty-Four

BBC
Wales - TV

By the time Em and I were seated at the kitchen table in our new St. David's home later that evening, our initial shock about the name Emily Muff had morphed into outrage. "I still can't believe that our so-called friends in Family would give our duo a name with such a sleazy connotation," Janet moaned. I nodded my head, and told her that I was also upset to learn that we'd been so frigging naïve. Rising from my seat, I walked over to the window and glanced outside. The setting sun was casting hues of purple, orange and gold on the trees in the yard, but my mood was dark and angry. "Listen, Moo!" Janet was saying. "I think that the main issue is whether we're going to keep our duo's name—or change it to something else." I swiveled back in her direction.

"When I first heard the name Emily Muff, I liked it, because it was unique—and had a quirky sound," I replied. "At this point, however, I'd be more inclined to change it." Janet agreed with me.

However, we both knew that word was already out about our chick rock duo, and Lotus was, no doubt, already making arrangements for us to go on tour with Family. The two of us were silent for several minutes, and then suddenly Janet began to laugh.

"And don't forget that we've already been calling each other Em and Moo, as well!"

After much discussion, my bandmate and I decided to keep the name Emily Muff, but we were determined to question the Leicester Lads when we saw them next. In the weeks that followed, our duo continued to write songs and rehearse in its St. David's hideaway. Em and I also took some time to explore the local sights, including St. David's Cathedral and the cliffs overlooking Carfey Bay. Soon, we heard from Meic Stevens, who invited our duo to make a guest appearance on his special program. It was to be filmed at his farmhouse in Solva, South Wales, and aired on BBC Wales-TV at a later date. The two of us gladly accepted his invitation, and began prepping for the show. Since it seemed as though Meic primarily performed ballads, we chose one of our duo's softer songs for its premier television appearance.

On the day of the filming Meic greeted Em and me at his home. He then introduced us to his lady, Tessa, and their two daughters before leading us into a room that had been set up for our duo's portion of the television shoot. Janet and I set our instruments down, and Meic began to chuckle. "Now remember, ladies, I want this show to have an informal feel, so don't start acting like a couple of pumped-up rock stars."

Soon, the BBC Wales-TV production crew began to arrive. The ground floor of Meic's house became a hub of activity, as a labyrinth of cameras and sound equipment was being set up. "Girls! Please take your places so we can get a preliminary sound-check," a member of the crew requested. As Em and I stepped up to the two mic stands that had been set up for us, I was careful not to trip over the electrical cables that were snaking along the floor. Tessa mouthed the words "Good Luck" to us before she hustled her children out of the room.

"Listen up, everybody! Let's do a take!" the director shouted, and a hush fell over the room. Janet and I were suddenly bathed in bright lights, and I felt a trickle of sweat run down my neck. Members of the film crew then instructed us to wait for them to cue us in. They also requested that we pause for several seconds before our duo began to play. We nodded, and Janet re-checked the tuning of her guitar. After that, the two of us stepped up to the microphones, and we were told that the cameras were ready to roll. My heart did a series of mini flip-flops as Janet poised her guitar pick over the fret board of her guitar, and I raised an ocarina to my lips.

"One, two, three, four . . ." my bandmate began to count, and our duo launched into the beginning notes of our song "Return and Beyond."

"Thought-seekers, mind-freakers
Joking and singing,
And hoping to bring
The sun to the earth . . ."

133

As we continued to play, I was swept away by the magic of the moment, and my pre-gig jitters disappeared. Janet seemed to get in the groove, as well, and our harmonies blended beautifully together.

"Cut!" the director of the TV shoot yelled after Emily Muff's performance. One by one, the glaring lights were switched off, and the BBC Wales-TV crew began sorting through their gear. I felt an acute sense of loss as my body came crashing down from its adrenaline rush. As Janet and I began packing up our instruments, various members of the TV crew complimented us on our music. Meic Stevens approached us, as well, congratulating our duo on its premier television appearance. Em and I thanked him for the opportunity to be on his show, and followed "The Welsh Dylan" into an adjacent room—where he was to perform his set. As my friend and I listened to him play several minutes later, I felt honored that Meic had chosen our female duo to be featured on his BBC Wales-TV program.

It had been an amazing opportunity—and one I knew we would never forget.

Chapter Twenty-Five

Blind Faith

After the filming of our duo for BBC Wales-TV, Em and I continued to work diligently on our music at the cottage in St. David's. Things were moving right along—until I was unexpectedly hospitalized for appendicitis, and our rehearsals came to a screeching halt. I was grateful that Janet visited me whenever she could while I was recuperating at the medical facility. This was no easy feat; we had no car, which meant that she had to resort to hitchhiking the thirty-odd miles round trip. Several friends offered her the occasional lift, but I still felt bad that she had been subjected to this unexpected ordeal.

Robin Williamson of the Incredible String Band came to visit as well, sneaking his dog Leafy into the medical building one day. While he was there, Robin informed us that the Incredible String Band was about to depart for America on tour. He invited our duo to stay at his home, Tryhidd, in Brynbarian, Wales, while his band was away. It seemed as though this had come at an opportune time, and we accepted Robin's generous invitation. Janet started packing up our belongings at once. On the day that I was discharged from the medical facility, Robin's friend and housemate, Nicky, helped move us from St. David's to Tryhidd.

The Incredible String Band's home was a lovely two-story house surrounded by the lush, green countryside. I spotted what looked like several ancient Megalithic stones in a nearby meadow. Inside, the front room was cozy, and a hand-painted sign announcing that the adjoining area was "Likky's Kitchen" hung in a prominent place. An array of art and hand-crafted items decorated the various shelves and windowsills throughout the house. By that time, I was healing well from my surgery, and I was looking forward to basking in the peaceful ambiance of Tryhidd. However, Robin's friend made an unwelcome advance to one of us on the day we had arrived there, and the tension in the house quickly escalated. Finally, Nicky and Leafy moved out, and Janet and I resumed rehearsals.

One afternoon, Em and I received a letter from a friend in Chelsea informing us that John Weider, a former bassist with Eric Burdon and the Animals, had replaced Ric Grech in the band Family. This missive also mentioned that the new super-group Blind Faith, which included our buddy Ric, was booked to play a debut concert in London's Hyde Park on June 7, 1969. The letter had arrived at Tryhidd the *day before* Ric's debut gig, but we decided to surprise him anyway by showing up at the event. Em and I hitch-hiked to the town of Carmarthen, traveling the rest of the way to London by the overnight Mail train. Once we arrived in the city, we headed to Hyde Park, and the Serpentine.

Over 100,000 Blind Faith fans were already jam-packed into the area, eagerly awaiting the opportunity to get a glimpse of the Clapton/Winwood/Baker/Grech super-group perform.

Em and I had to dodge flying Frisbees, side-step around baby prams, and tiptoe between spread-out blankets as we cut a swath through the crowd en route to the backstage area. At one point we were surrounded by a group of Hari Krishna dancers who were dressed in flowing, saffron robes. "Man! After being so far away in Wales, I'm in culture shock!' I exclaimed.

"Me, too! Do you think Ric will remember us?"

"I think so . . . but now that he's made it to superstar status, it's more a question of whether he'll *choose* to acknowledge us," I replied with a grin.

When Janet and I finally arrived at the roped-off artist's area, we spotted our friend Ric—and a rush of emotion coursed through me. Em must have felt something similar; she sprinted ahead while shouting out the bassist's name. When I caught up with my bandmate, I saw that her eyes were moist as she hugged our long-lost buddy. "Ohh! It's so fantastic to see you again, Ric," my friend cried into the bassist's neck. After the two of them finally pulled apart, he spotted me, and another round of hugs began. Once the three of us had finally regained our composure, we filled Ric in on the status of Emily Muff, including how we had traveled all the way from Wales in order to be present at Blind Faith's debut concert.

"You bloody twits didn't have to go to all that trouble to get here!"

our former Lots Road buddy replied. "Still . . . I'm worth it!" he added with a chuckle. The two of us continued to hang out with Ric until a guy from Blackhill Enterprises, the show's promoter, appeared on the scene, and whisked the bassist away for a series of publicity photos.

When Blind Faith finally appeared onstage, Steve Winwood led the band in a series of numbers that included "Do What You Like," "Presence of the Lord," and "Well All Right." As they performed, I marveled at the way in which Eric Clapton's lead guitar solos soared out over the Serpentine, while drummer Ginger Baker's amazing rhythms provided the backbone for the band. Most of all, I was proud of Ric; his technical prowess was very much in evidence, proving he had what it took to be a bona fide member of a rock 'n' roll super-group.

Later that day, Em and I ran into several other friends of ours near the Serpentine. They told us that while we were away in Wales, Mick Jagger had been living with Marianne Faithful in Cheyne Walk, the Who were performing their rock opera "Tommy" in America, and the Beatles had released a single called "Get Back." Janet and I returned to Wales the day after the Blind Faith concert, and resumed rehearsals. However, we were suddenly finding it difficult to concentrate on our music. It was clear that the two of us had been metaphorically bitten by the London bug, and we were eager to return to the city.

Chapter Twenty-Six

Butterflies for Brian

Although Em and I were chomping at the bit to move back to London, we decided to remain at Tryhidd for several more weeks. During this time, we wrapped up our rehearsal sessions, and began packing up our belongings. My friend and I were busy sorting through our things one morning when we heard the shocking news on the String Band's radio that musician Brian Jones of the Rolling Stones had reportedly died in a swimming pool accident. The newscaster also mentioned that the Stones had arranged to play a Free Open-Air Concert in Brian's memory on July 5th near the Serpentine in Hyde Park. Upon hearing the news, Em and I arranged for our friend Nick Laurie to move us back to London in time for this important event. The three of us made the journey to the city squished in his sporty car, along with our luggage and his Irish Setter pup. With Nick's permission, Janet and I also arranged to stay for a while at his penthouse pad in Addison Gardens, and he graciously allowed us to store our belongings there during that time.

True to our word, Janet and I were among the mourners gathered to honor musician Brian Jones at the Free Open-Air Concert. Although the memorial show was obviously a solemn occasion, I was secretly pleased that Family had been booked to appear on the bill, along with King Crimson, Third Ear Band, Battered Ornaments, Screw, and Alexis Korner's New Church Band. As Em and I made our way through the more than 250,000 fans in attendance, she pointed towards one side of the stage. "Look! There's Family over there!" I glanced in the direction she had indicated, and saw that vocalist Roger Chapman was chatting with his bandmates, guitarist Charlie Whitney and drummer Rob Townsend. There was also another guy standing with them who I didn't recognize.

Once Roger spotted us, he waved us over. We raced in his direction and, soon, Janet and I were encircled by all four of them. It felt great to be back in the Family fold, and all thoughts of confronting them about the name they'd given our duo momentarily disappeared from my mind. "Well! Well!" Roger exclaimed. "If it isn't Em and Moo come back to London." As he spoke, I noticed he had the requisite towel draped around his neck in anticipation of his upcoming, sweat-drenched performance. Charlie grinned at the two of us.

"Yeah! It's about time you chicks showed up," he chimed in. Janet and I were then introduced to bassist John Weider, the newest addition to Family. Although John seemed quite shy, he had a friendly smile, and we chatted with him for a bit. Then Roger asked Em and me whether we had come back to London for good. Janet nodded, and told him that we were staying with a friend. As she spoke, Family's manager, Tony Gourvish, arrived on the scene, and joined in the mini-reunion.

"Ready to go on tour, girls?" the businessman asked. It was obvious that Lotus was still interested in Emily Muff opening shows for Family, and he arranged for us to meet with him the following day. I barely managed to contain my excitement at the thought of hitting the road with this popular, underground rock band. Several minutes later, Family's set was announced. Janet and I made our way back through the crowd, and managed to score a terrific spot near the front of the stage.

As we watched the concert, my emotions vacillated between feeling elated at the prospect of Emily Muff's impending tour, and the urge to weep for the tragic loss of Brian Jones. As soon as the Leicester Lads appeared onstage, the crowd began to cheer. Roger Chapman's voice soared out over the Serpentine, and I smiled to myself. Performances by Family were always awesome, no matter the occasion, and I couldn't wait for Emily Muff to hit the road as its opening act. Janet reached over and squeezed my hand. It was obvious that she was equally excited at the prospect of our chick rock duo touring the British music circuit with Family.

Later, when the Rolling Stones made an appearance during the finale of the show, an eerie hush descended over the crowd. It was easy to imagine the ethereal presence of Brian Jones hovering over the mass of humanity that had gathered in his honor, and I found it difficult to keep my tears in check. My mind kept drifting back to the time when I had met him at the Phone Booth Club in Manhattan when I was sixteen. His recent passing was a tragedy, and I felt fortunate to have had the opportunity to tell him in person how much I admired his artistry.

Even though the Rolling Stones played an impressive set at Brian's memorial concert, there were moments when Mick Jagger's vocal delivery sounded a bit restrained. Dressed in an outfit reminiscent of a Greek tunic, he read the poem, "Adonis" by Shelly ("Peace, peace! He is not dead, he doth not sleep/He hath awakened from the dream of life."). At one point, a hoard of white butterflies had been released into the air . . . but many of them floated listlessly onto the stage. When the concert wrapped up, Em and I returned to the backstage area. Despite all the groupies hanging out there, we were able to rendezvous with members of Family once more. "You birds aren't planning to disappear on us again, are you?" one of them asked us.

"Nah!" I replied. "The only place we're headed is on the road with you guys!"

"Then you'd better get your bums on over to Bradgate Bush first thing in the morning, and meet with Tony," vocalist Roger announced. As he spoke, Family's roadie, Harvey, appeared and informed members of the band that their van would be departing for their home in Chelsea shortly. Roger waved good-bye to us, and joined his bandmates as they hustled towards their vehicle. Suddenly, I realized that Janet and I had failed to confront them about the name they had given our duo.

"Hey! About the name Emily Muff . . ." I called out after them. Several members of Family whirled around and began to chuckle.

"You have to admit," one of them shouted in reply, "the name's got a funky flavor!" Janet and I rolled our eyes at them, but neither of us followed the Leicester Lads as they hurried towards their vehicle.

Later that night, Em and I discussed our conflicting emotions about the racy name Family had dubbed our duo. After all, if it was so unacceptable to us . . . then why had *neither* of us confronted members of family until the concert was over, and they had been heading towards their van.

It was obvious that we needed to decide whether to:

1. Confront them again about the name they'd given our duo.

2. Keep our band's name, Emily Muff.

3. Change the name ourselves (but this late in the game?).

Although Janet and I had obviously been shocked to learn the connotation of the word "muff," we also knew that our duo had an important meeting with Tony the following day. We were hoping that, during this appointment, he would offer to become our manager.

There was a lot at stake . . .

"At this point, I'm not so sure it's a good idea for us to march into our meeting with Lotus tomorrow and insist that our duo's name be changed," I observed.

"Yeah, I know. We're in a tough spot here, especially since he may have already booked us on Family's upcoming tour. And he might have ordered posters, concert programs, and Melody Maker ads with the name Emily Muff on them, as well," Janet replied.

The two of us continued to weigh the options as to whether we should rock the boat at our upcoming meeting with Lotus by demanding a name change for our band. Or were we willing to accept the name Emily Muff—and our monikers, too? Family had been calling us "Em and Moo" from the day they named our duo back at Lots Road, and we had embraced these nicknames among ourselves.

After much thought, Janet and I decided to keep our quirky nicknames, and the name Emily Muff. After all, we kind of liked them anyway. Most of all, however, an offer to hit the road with one of Britain's hottest underground bands would be a dream-come-true for our chick rock duo.

"So, we've made our FINAL decision eh, Moo?

"Looks like it, Em!" I replied and, soon, we were sorting through our clothing, searching for some groovy outfits to wear at Emily Muff's all-important meeting with Tony the following day.

Chapter Twenty-Seven

Twin Telecasters

Janet and I arrived promptly at Bradgate Bush the next day for our appointment with Tony Gourvish. During this meeting, Lotus offered to provide representation for our duo, and said that arrangements were being made to book Emily Muff as Family's intro act on its upcoming tour. It was final confirmation of this incredible opportunity, and the two of us were thrilled at the news! Tony waited patiently for our shrieks to subside, and then he cleared his throat.

"Now, listen up, girls! Since your duo is about to go on tour with Family, you obviously can't continue to call me something so asinine as 'Lotus' any longer." Although his vocal intonation sounded rather austere, I could tell from the twitching motions his mouth was making that he was having difficulty suppressing a chuckle.

"No problem, *Lotus!*" I replied with a grin. "Since you've done so much for our duo, I'm sure we can honor your request." Our manager grabbed a decorative pillow from his couch, which he hurled playfully in my direction. It landed at my feet, and I cracked a smile. It was obvious that Em and I had no intention of dropping the nickname "Lotus," and Tony finally broke down and laughed along with us.

After the meeting with our new, official manager had wrapped up that day, Janet and I purchased the album "Family Entertainment." It was about time that we owned a copy for ourselves, especially since it had been released in early March while we were still rehearsing in Wales. This album by Family had soared into the Top Ten on the UK Album Chart, and the song "The Weaver's Answer" was also released as a single.

In the meantime, many exciting events had been taking place in the music scene. By August 2, 1969 the Rolling Stones had released "Honky Tonk Woman," and Crosby, Stills, and Nash had issued their single "Marrakech Express." Em and I had seen Bob Dylan perform at the Isle of Wight on August 6th and nine days later, the Woodstock Festival in upstate New York ushered in a new era of mega-festivals.

Before our duo was to go on tour, our manager booked Emily Muff for its first photo shoot. It was to be held at one of London's spacious parks, and pictures from that professional photo session were to be used for publicity purposes. They would appear in all of the Family/Emily Muff concert programs on our tours throughout Great Britain, he assured us.

This was a perfect opportunity for Emily Muff to make itself known!

The photo shoot took place in early fall on a day that was sunny, but a bit chilly. Em and I had dressed up for the occasion, yet we were a little uncertain as to how to go about posing for the camera. Lotus must have sensed this. All of a sudden, he began tossing colorful leaves in our direction, and cracking corny jokes. His silly antics worked; the camera caught me laughing wildly at his playful banter, and the photo that was selected had an informal ambiance. I didn't consider it to be especially flattering, but that particular publicity shot of Emily Muff sitting amidst the leaves became a special, memorable photo nonetheless. For me, it represents the closeness and camaraderie that we shared with our manager, Tony Gourvish, on that all-important day.

In the meantime, Janet and I did not want to overstay our welcome at Nick's penthouse pad. So, we moved into a communal house in Finchley, at 11 Waverly Grove in North London. Other members of this rather eclectic household included an American artist, Jim, entrepreneur Paddy, a couple named Jackie and Anthony, and a young American woman, Holly. We had only been living there a short while when Janet flew back to New York to visit her parents. Em's mother and father were very supportive of her music career in Britain. They had already spent time visiting her in Britain, and now she had returned from her trip to New York with two brand-new, cream-colored Fender Telecaster electric guitars that her parents had generously purchased for Emily Muff.

I was grateful that Janet's family was rooting for our duo—especially since my mother and father were the polar opposite. My parents continued to express their dislike of my involvement in the rock music scene. I knew they traveled all over the world to a variety of academic conferences, yet they'd not once visited me since I'd moved across the pond. Moreover, they had certainly not bothered to show support by gifting us anything because that's how much they disapproved of my rock career.

With our two brand new Telecasters in hand, Janet and I continued to rehearse for our upcoming tour with Family—knowing full well that Emily Muff would soon be put to the ultimate test!

Chapter Twenty-Eight

The Marquee Club

As it turned out, Emily Muff and its flute, Hohner Blues Harps, and twin Telecaster guitars were, indeed, put to the test when we opened a show for Family at Mother's Club in Birmingham. After that successful gig, our chick rock duo was booked for its official, premier London appearance at the Marquee Club on Tuesday, October 7, 1969. Emily Muff was to open for the bands Family and Stone the Crows, and we were super excited! After all, this was *the* Marquee Club, where famous bands like the Rolling Stones and the Who had made their debut gigs.

Entrepreneur Paddy from our communal house drove Emily Muff rock-star style in his elegant Rolls Royce to the club. He also volunteered to carry our guitars into the venue. When we arrived at the Marquee, Paddy looked for a place to park, while Janet and I made our way towards the backstage entrance. As we went up the steps, I noticed that a burly bouncer was blocking the doorway. He scowled at the two of us, and announced that only musicians were allowed beyond that point.

"But we're opening for the band Family tonight," I explained. The bouncer snickered, and told us that we could *open* for the band later when we got back to their house. It was obvious that he had mistaken us for a couple of groupie chicks, and I flashed him a haughty look that was filled with disgust. Em seemed pissed off by his sleazy remark, as well. Although we continued to insist that our rock duo was booked as Family's support group that night, the bouncer refused to budge from his position blocking the doorway.

Luckily, Roger Chapman of Family was already inside the club, and happened to be passing by the backstage door. When he heard us arguing with the security guard, the vocalist opened the door, and called out to us. "All set for your gig tonight, girls?" he asked. The bully backed away, and Roger tugged the two of us inside the club. After escorting Em and me further into the venue, he began lecturing us on the need for our duo to stick close to Family when we were on tour. He went on to explain that many blokes were "So fucking high, they wouldn't think twice about pulling you girls."

"Pulling?" I muttered under my breath. Roger rolled his eyes.

"Christ, didn't they teach you *anything* in America?" Family's vocalist went on to explain that *pulling* meant screwing someone, and I made a mental note to remember the term. Next, Janet and I followed Roger into the dressing room area. Several members of Family were standing there in various stages of undress. I politely averted my eyes but not before taking note that some of them were

150

wearing skimpy, bikini briefs. I leaned towards Em and whispered, "What? No separate dressing room for women?"

"I guess not, Moo," she answered. We soon confirmed that there were no separate dressing rooms for females at the club, so we made our way towards the ladies' room. It had never occurred to us that we'd be expected to share a dressing room with our male musician buddies. Or that we'd have any trouble getting into the club in the first place. "I sure hope we won't have to put up with this kind of crap at every gig on this tour," Janet remarked.

"That's for sure! Does Lotus expect us to parade around in our panties in front of Family?"

A cluster of dolly birds had already staked out the mirror in the ladies' room. They were busy applying false eyelashes, and gobs of make-up on their faces. I slipped into an empty stall, closed the door, and felt a flood of vulnerability overwhelm me. So far, Emily Muff's premier London engagement was off to a rocky start. I had assumed that Janet and I would be free to focus all of our energy on performing our original songs. Instead, there was no dressing room for females, and we were holed up in some grimy lavatory, wishing someone had clued us in to the fact that we'd be fending off sleazy bouncers at the backstage door. Many female musicians/singers married (or shacked up with) their managers or a member of their band. I was beginning to wonder whether these unions were, in fact, love matches—or based on the woman's need for protection from the seedier side of the macho music scene.

When I emerged from the stall several minutes later, even more groupies had invaded the ladies' room. So, Em and I left the loo in search of a private place backstage to call our own. We managed to locate an empty, closet-sized area and promptly set it up as a make-shift dressing room. Even though it had no mirrors, chairs or hangers, we managed to make ourselves performance-ready. By the time our guitars and harmonicas were set up onstage, my bandmate and I had been told that Emily Muff had "Five minutes 'til show time!"

In less than that, we were ready to rock!

From my vantage point in the "wings," I could see that Emily Muff's Telecaster guitars and a pair of microphones had been set up center stage. Family's mega-stacks of Marshall amps were placed near the back. Since there had not been an opportunity for our duo to have a pre-gig sound check, I hoped that Emily Muff's Tele's were in tune, and the PA volume adjusted. Janet leaned towards me, and whispered the age-old phrase "Break a leg," and I mouthed this saying back to her. As I was wiping the palms of my hands on my mini-dress, the emcee stepped onstage.

"Ladies and Gentlemen . . . presenting two lovely little ladies all the way from America . . . Emily Muff!" he announced. My jaw clenched at such a corny introduction. Well! My bandmate and I had news for everyone! These "lovely little ladies" were about to show the London music scene that Emily Muff was neither a ditsy little duo nor a bunch of fluffed-up hype. As we rushed onstage, the intense heat from the spotlights overhead enveloped us. A ripple of applause wended its way towards the stage, and the realization that

Emily Muff was no longer rehearsing in the privacy of its Finchley Road commune hit me full-force.

This was the *real* thing!

Janet and I swung the straps of our cream-colored Telecaster guitars over our shoulders. While the audience waited for us to begin, a hush descended over the club. Suddenly, the silence was broken by a series of cat-calls from a couple of blokes standing near the back of the venue.

"Hey baby! Let it all hang out!"

"Come on, girls! Give it to me!"

I pretended not to hear their snide remarks as I whipped my long, blonde hair behind my shoulders. Em and I checked our Telecasters to make sure they were still in tune, but their volume was so loud, screeching feedback ricocheted throughout the club. Once the decibel level had been adjusted, we stepped up to our microphones. "Hello everyone!" my bandmate began. "It's great to be here tonight! The first song we're going to play is an instrumental called 'Essence.'"

Her announcement was followed by another series of feedback noises that sent the roadies scrambling, a second time, to adjust the sound. While our duo waited for the crew to fix this latest glitch, Janet and I re-checked our tuning. Luckily, there were no more electrical issues, and we began playing our first number. Soon, I felt cocky enough to glance up from my instrument and visually scan the crowd.

Although I had expected the audience to be grooving on our sound, I noticed that many of the male patrons were watching us with their faces tilted at an angle. It appeared as though they were more focused on catching a glimpse of panty under our skirts than listening to the music. Although I knew that a band's image was ultra-important to the moguls of the music industry, I longed for members of the audience to groove on our powerful bar chords, lead guitar, dynamic vocal delivery, and rockin' harmonica solos instead of ogling Emily Muff as an erotic novelty. Our female duo had already been saddled with a suggestive name. We had no wish to further emphasize the hype.

As Emily Muff concluded its set, Janet and I shouted into our microphones, "Good night, everybody! Thank you very much!" Applause echoed throughout the Marquee and we bowed, once again. My bandmate unstrapped her guitar, while I pocketed my Hohner harmonicas. The two of us waved to the crowd, and then we dashed off the stage.

"'How'd it go?" Roger asked as he stepped out of Family's dressing room and cornered the two of us in the backstage area. As he spoke, roadie Harvey handed Family's vocalist a towel, which he promptly draped over his shoulders. Em and I mentioned how the screeching feedback had thrown us a bit at the beginning of our set. Roger told us that our duo would acquire more confidence as we gained experience touring. Janet and I thanked him for his support, and we watched as he made his way towards the stage. The remaining members of Family soon followed, and the roar of the crowd was deafening as the Leicester Lads rushed onstage.

The following day, Tony Gourvish contacted Janet and me, and announced that he had been pleased with Emily Muff's performance at the Marquee Club. Lotus went on to say that he'd been busy making arrangements for our duo to continue touring with Family.

Emily Muff would soon be embarking on its first UK tour!

Chapter Twenty-Nine

Colston Hall

Em and I were proud that our female rock duo had made its official London debut at the Marquee Club. Even though a couple of electrical glitches had threatened to throw us for a loop, the two of us had carried on. We were especially looking forward to one of our upcoming gigs, at Colston Hall in Bristol, where our duo had been booked to open the sold-out concert.

My bandmate and I were always searching for ways to learn from our experiences. If we could have changed one thing about Emily Muff's gig at the Marquee Club, it would have been our run-in with the bouncer at the backstage door. It was obviously too late to alter his boorish behavior that night. However, we did have the power to devise some sort of "sleaze-bag prevention plan" that made sure something similar would not happen again. In thinking things through we reasoned that, if the two of us were to carry our guitars into the various concert halls, it might make it less likely that we'd be stopped by groupie-screening bouncers in the future. And so, we came up with a plan.

<u>Em and Moo's Sleaze-Bag Prevention Plan:</u>

1) Roadie Harvey hands us our Telecasters when we arrive at concert halls.

2) We approach the backstage door (armed with proof that we're musicians).

3) The bouncer/stagehand lets us into the venue without question.

4) Once we're safely inside, Family's roadie intercepts us again.

5) Harvey sets our guitars up onstage, in time for our pre-gig soundcheck.

As it turned out, roadie Harvey was eager to help us out, and he readily agreed to our plan of action. So, when we arrived in Family's van outside the backstage entrance at Colston Hall on the day of the show, the three of us implemented our scheme.

First, Janet and I exited the vehicle.

We grinned at our roadie, and he handed us our twin Telecaster guitars.

Em and I then carried these instruments to the backstage entrance . . .

Where the stagehand waved us through (can't be groupies, they've got guitars).

"Hello, girls! Your dressing room's down the hall," the young man informed us. As we sidled past him, I lifted my chin a couple of inches and flashed him a smile. We handed our guitars to Harvey, then located our dressing room and went inside. Janet and I were excited to be opening a show at the illustrious Colston Hall, with its changing room for females that featured makeup vanities with rows of lights, Hollywood style. It was obvious that a venue as renowned and spacious as this would come equipped with dressing rooms for both genders. However, this was the first concert hall that Emily Muff had been officially booked to play—and having a changing room all to ourselves felt extra special.

I thought about how Em and I had struggled to rig up a make-shift dressing room at the Marquee Club. We had even spoken with Tony about our dilemma after the show, but he had told us that there was nothing he could do. According to him, there probably wasn't a separate changing room because there hadn't been a need for one in the smaller venues.

In many ways, the world of rock still seemed very much a boys' club.

When Lotus knocked on our Colston Hall dressing room door several minutes later, I slammed back from my reverie. He stepped inside saying, "Listen up, Em and Moo! You need to get your bums onstage for your soundcheck." Janet and I glanced in the mirror a final time, and then followed our manager into the theater. As we gazed out over the sea of empty seats from our vantage point in the wings, I pointed to the topmost row and exclaimed, "Wow! This place is humongous." Em began to laugh.

"Yeah! Looks like we're going to have to jack up the volume on our Tele's so people sitting all the way up in the balcony can hear every single note, eh, Moo?" We emerged from the wings, and began wandering around the stage. Suddenly, the spotlights were being tested, enveloping the two of us in a rainbow of colors.

"Hurry up and grab your guitars, girls!" our manager bellowed from the middle of the theater, where he was now sitting with the sound engineer. Em and I hurriedly retrieved our instruments, and hustled towards the microphone stands that had been set up for us center stage. While we adjusted their heights, the soundman called out to us.

"Now listen up, ladies! We need you to play a few bars of your songs so we can get a proper volume level." I jokingly sauntered over to a stack of Marshall amps, and pretended to jack up the volume. Em cracked a smile before she began counting in the tempo.

"One, two three, four . . ."

I rushed back to the mic, and joined her in the opening bars of our band's first number. Since the balance sounded fine, we continued playing a mini-medley of Emily Muff originals. Although the sound crew had to make several adjustments when the highest notes of my harmonica solo set off a series of feedback noises, everything else went without a hitch. Next, it was time for Family's soundcheck, and we exited the stage. Em and I watched from the wings as lead guitarist, John "Charlie" Whitney straddled his twin-neck Gibson guitar and ripped out a series of flashy riffs that ricocheted off the interior walls of Colston Hall. Soon afterwards, the Leicester Lads were playing their song, "See Through Windows." As I listened to their music, I glanced out over the empty rows of seats, and envisioned Emily Muff playing to over two hundred Family fans later that evening.

The time flew by. Before we knew it, roadie Harvey was knocking at our dressing room door, telling us that the concert was, indeed, sold out—and we had five minutes until showtime. Em and I made last-minute touches to our hair and, by the time Harvey turned up again with a final warning, I was ready to rock out in my red velvet mini-dress, purple embroidered satin jacket, and knee-high leather boots. I grinned at my bandmate and said, "Okay! Let's get this show on the road!"

"Emily Muff's already on the road, you nitwit," Janet reminded me, and the two of us burst out laughing. I then grabbed my Hohner harps and guitar picks before following her out of the dressing room. The heels of my boots made a series of clicking sounds as the two of us made a beeline through the backstage area. When we arrived in the wings, the distinct hum of the crowd could be heard. I peeked out through a chink in the curtains and saw that the concert hall was jam-packed!

Em and I glanced at each other, and I gave her a thumbs-up signal. By that time, our manager had stepped up to one of the microphones onstage and was asking the audience to give Emily Muff a special welcome. His request was followed by a wave of applause. Lotus disappeared in the wings and I rushed alongside Janet towards the Telecaster guitars and the two mic stands awaiting us near the front of the stage.

After grabbing our guitars, we swung their straps over our shoulders and poised our picks over their fretboards. Suddenly, the stage was bathed in a blinding array of lights, and we both blinked momentarily in the glare. I could see members of the audience in the first several rows of seats, but the rest of the concert hall interior was hidden in the shadows. Despite Emily Muff's limited vantage point, I could feel the audience's raw energy as it sliced through the arena.

As we began to play, it felt fantastic to be sharing our music with the audience. Janet and I were totally in sync, and our songs soared throughout Colston hall. When the final notes faded away, the capacity crowd rose from their seats and were giving Emily Muff a standing ovation!

Em and I took our bows, smiled at the crowd, and called out, "Thank you very much!" before we exited the stage. The two of us ran straight into Roger, who had been watching our duo from the wings. This time he didn't ask us how our performance went.

Instead, he clapped us on our backs and said, "You chicks are going to be a hard act to follow!"

Chapter Thirty

Touring
Twists and Turns

After the concert at Colston Hall, we purchased a 12-string Rickenbacker electric guitar, and added it to our lineup as Emily Muff continued touring with Family from Plymouth to Glasgow. Our duo was becoming more widely known in the rock music circuit, gaining a measure of acceptance among its male counterparts along the way. Musicians John Weider and Poli Palmer were members of Family now, and it was an honor for our duo to be traveling down the motorways in the white van, performing gig after gig. Janet and I were especially pleased to discover that Family had dedicated their latest album, "A Song for Me" to "You, Emily Muff . . ." and others, whose names I recognized. Family's friendship with our duo, and all the times we opened concerts, playing our music in front of an enthusiastic crowd definitely made my heart soar.

And Roger was right; we did gain confidence with experience.

Most of the time, it was Family and Emily Muff who appeared on the bill. However, there were other instances when we opened concerts for Family that also featured multiple acts—including big-name bands such as Yes, the Nice, Steppenwolf, and the Move. When our duo was booked on the same bill as Yes, I enjoyed standing in the wings, grooving on Jon Anderson's crystal-clear voice and the band's innovative songs. After these shows, Em and I would talk shop with our musician buddies and joke around with Tony Kaye about our Lots Road days.

As our rock duo continued touring, it became clear that Family's former bassist, Ric, had been spot-on when he told us about the rigors of life on the road. Even though traveling around Great Britain had become a way of life for us, it had lost some of its initial appeal. After all, it wasn't much fun being jam-packed for hours in a van loaded down with heavy equipment. The only respite might be a series of quick bathroom breaks and barely enough time to grab a bite to eat at one of the transport cafes along the motorways. Em and I had also become accustomed to living out of our suitcases, and attending the requisite Scotch 'n' Coke post-gig parties at the various local pubs.

The two of us also quickly learned that a life on the road could be quite unpredictable at times. On one occasion, our duo was rockin' away in the middle of its set when the electricity suddenly went out in the concert hall.

The colorful spotlights illuminating the stage had blinked off in an instant. Except for the emergency/exit lights, Emily Muff had been left standing onstage in the middle of a blackout.

We both knew that the show must go on, so we jumped into action. After unstrapping our Telecasters, we asked the roadies to bring us two acoustic guitars. In no time, my bandmate and I were playing a pair of borrowed guitars, and belting out the song that we'd been singing before the lights went out. Through it all, the two of us had barely missed a beat. After the lights in the concert hall came back on several minutes later, the crowd showered us with a chorus of rousing cheers, in honor of Emily Muff's impromptu, unplugged performance.

Another time, when Family and Emily Muff had arrived at a different concert hall, we discovered that the piano onstage was missing several, strategic keys. It was sorely out of tune, as well, and the two of us had to do a last-minute rearranging of our setlist before the show. As soon as our duo returned to London, we purchased a reliable, portable electronic keyboard for our use when Emily Muff was on the road.

Then there was the crazy situation that occurred when I was in the middle of a routine dental cleaning in London. Without warning, roadie Harvey suddenly appeared in the doorway. He explained to me that Family and Emily Muff had been booked at the last minute to play a gig up north, and we needed to leave immediately. The expression on the dentist's face was priceless as the burly roadie hauled me from the room—with the white dental bib still dangling from its chain around my neck.

Despite the rigors of the road and its unpredictable glitches, Em and I would not have traded a chick rocker's life for anything—and we marveled at how far our duo had come since we first met members of Family outside their Lots Road home. Janet and I enjoyed the fun times, too, joking around with our musician buddies as the van barreled down the motorways on our way to the various concert halls. It was a heady feeling to be touring with this popular underground rock band. When I first heard Family's hit song "Second Generation Woman" come blasting over the radio airways, Janet and I had been riding with them in their van on the way to a Family/Emily Muff concert. Roadie Harvey was driving and, as the song played, he jacked up the volume, and then screeched the vehicle to a halt on the shoulder of the motorway. As the Leicester Lads and Emily Muff continued to cheer, Family's van was literally rockin' on its chassis while we all sang along with the song.

Perhaps the most memorable moment for me on the touring circuit took place during a sold-out concert in the London area. As usual, our duo had opened the show for Family, and I was rockin' out on my Hohner harp. I glanced out into the audience, and spotted Mick Jagger and Keith Richards standing on one side of the theater. Their faces were illuminated by the glow of the Exit sign as they watched Emily Muff's performance.

The presence of the Glimmer Twins watching us play sent my adrenaline into overdrive, and I nearly dropped my harmonica. But I boldly swiveled in their direction, instead, and kept my cool by pretending that I was playing an informal solo for these megastars.

Chapter Thirty-One

Identity Dilemma

Later, when Emily Muff had been on the touring circuit for quite some time we learned about the rumors that had been circulating throughout the music scene about us. According to one report, we were lesbians who were flaunting our butch identity by emulating Great Britain's big-wig, male rockers. Other rumormongers were spreading the story that my bandmate and I had bedded the entire Family entourage, and we loved to fondle the fretboards of our "erected" guitars.

Our life was a far cry from the racy existence it was made out to be, and rumors such as these were simply untrue. We had no desire to be boxed into any one particular niche, either. After all, Em and I were primarily focused upon our quest for success—without compromising our principles. Our driving ambition was for audiences to be moved by our music, not by our tits and asses. We obviously knew that a band's image was important from a business standpoint.

However, when it came to the outfits we performed in, Janet and I had a penchant for esoteric, artsy attire, and we were reluctant to appear onstage all decked out in slinky, low-cut, or sparkly outfits.

Although the two of us were not focused on flaunting our female sexuality in an outrageous manner, it was clear that our duo's identity was metaphorically up for grabs by the general public.

Exactly what was Emily Muff, anyway?

Those who sought to compartmentalize our trailblazing chick rock duo and its music seemed quite mystified. It was obvious that Emily Muff was different from the various male/female lineups like the Mamas and the Papas, ABBA, or the Cowsills. We could hardly be classified as one of the girl groups such as the Supremes, either. Our duo did not perform covers nor were we moonlighting as back-up singers. Emily Muff was a rock 'n' roll rarity, a female duo on the British touring circuit whose members not only wrote all the band's material, but also provided instrumentation for the group with a variety of electric guitars, keyboards, blues harmonicas, and flute.

It was obvious that Great Britain had never seen anything quite like this Emily Muff, mini-American invasion!

While our female duo continued to be an intriguing mystery for many, Janet and I were maturing and growing in our understanding of the world of rock. Our naiveté had been steadily peeling away as we became more and more used to the ever-present scores of groupie chicks that were hanging out at the shows. The two of us were both amused and annoyed by the way our male musician buddies seemed to metamorphosize into blobs of putty around them.

When groupies arrived on the scene, it seemed as though all rational conversation would come to a screeching halt. Once they began wriggling their bums and flirting with the guys, my bandmate and I would hang out together in a far corner of the room and watch from the sidelines as our male buddies made asses of themselves by acting out silly, little antics in order to impress these groupies. As members of Family's touring entourage, Janet and I were privy to many of the comings and goings of these star-fuckers and their eager male rockers. We'd heard that Tony received fringe benefits, too, in the form of blow jobs from amorous fans in the back of Family's van.

Just a rumor, but a plausible one, it seemed.

Em and I teased Lotus about his supposedly clandestine adventures with these chicks while he, in turn, ribbed Emily Muff about the racy rumors that were circulating about us. Despite this merciless bantering back and forth, the three of us retained an underlying respect for each another. Our manager grooved on our music, and he had been one of the first to recognize Emily Muff's potential. He also served as a link between our duo and the business side of the music scene.

And that link would later become crucially important for Emily Muff.

Chapter Thirty-Two

Scouts in the Crowd

One afternoon, our manager requested that Em and I meet with him as soon as possible at his office. We suspected that something important was afoot, and the two of us were eager to hear "the scoop." So, we made sure to arrive promptly at Bradgate Bush. Once we were seated in Tony's office (opposite the pink, penis-shaped candle that was prominently displayed on his coffee table) he broke the news to us that Reprise Records had expressed an interest in signing Emily Muff to its mega record label.

Lotus waited patiently for our shrieks to subside before he went on to explain that scouts from this prestigious company were planning to attend Family and Emily Muff's upcoming concert at De Montfort Hall in Leicester. Their presence at the show was to celebrate both the release of Family's latest album, and to formally audition Emily Muff.

This was *the moment* that Em and I had been waiting for!

I glanced at my bandmate, and she promptly joined me in another series of rousing cheers, while Tony playfully rolled his eyes at us. Then our manager's face took on a more serious expression as he began warning us not to get too cocky. It was, after all, only an audition. Emily Muff clearly had a foot in the door, but we needed to remember that the recording contract was not yet in our hands.

Neither Janet nor I was feeling particularly cocky as we sat primping in our dressing room at De Montfort Hall in anticipation of our all-important audition for Reprise Records. "Where do you think the scouts will be sitting in the theater tonight, Em?" I mused. Janet shrugged her shoulders, and continued combing her dark, curly hair. After putting on a lacy slip, I reached for my dress that was on a nearby hanger. I had just pulled it down over my hips when Tony knocked on our door. He sauntered into the room, and began lecturing us on the importance of playing our best gig to date. Obviously, my bandmate and I did not need to be reminded that Emily Muff's career was at stake that very night, but we humored him anyway. Lotus motioned for us to follow him into a separate, lounge-like area backstage. As we entered the room, I noticed that members of Family were gathered around a table that had a cake displayed on it for the post-gig party. The word *Congratulations* had been written in colorful, hand-piped lettering to honor the release of their latest album, and I felt super-proud of our Lots Road buddies.

After Family and Emily Muff's pre-gig soundchecks had been completed, Roger sauntered over to Janet and me and wished us luck on our audition for Reprise. I felt my eyes mist over and was about to give him a quick hug when Harvey rushed over and told Em and me that we had five minutes before showtime. In less than that, my bandmate and I were standing center-stage, announcing our opening number.

Janet and I *always* poured our hearts out whenever we played our songs. On this particular night, however, images of scouts in the crowd kept flitting through my mind, and I felt a bit jittery as we performed another Emily Muff original:

> *"No use trying to shut him out,*
> *It's time you learned that when . . .*
> *Someone's been inside your head,*
> *They're never out again.*
> *Love is a circle,*
> *It has no end,*
> *It has no end . . ."*

After the show, I wondered whether our manager had heard anything about the results of Emily Muff's audition for Reprise. So, I searched for him backstage. Lotus wasn't in the room where the after-party was to be held and I headed for the auditorium, on the chance that I might find him there. No such luck. Family's roadies had already packed up the gear, and the arena was now empty. I shrugged my shoulders, and was about to return to the backstage area when one of the side doors of the concert hall banged open, and a crowd of preteen and adolescent boys sprinted in my direction.

"Oh! Look! There's one of them over there!"

"Come on, lads! It's Emily Muff!"

Several seconds later, the boys had arrived by my side. They were jostling one another in a tightly-knit pack. As they surged forward, I took a step back. "May I have your autograph?" one of them called out in a noticeably high-pitched tone of voice. I reached over, took the pen he was holding, signed his program, and pretended that being mobbed by a horde of fans was an everyday occurrence.

"Will you sign mine as well?" another boy was asking.

The crowd of male Emily Muff fans continued to ogle me in adoration, while I scribbled my name on their concert souvenirs. Soon, I had signed so many autographs that my wrist was throbbing. "Ohh! We think Emily Muff's absolutely *fab*, don't we lads?" a freckled-faced boy sighed. He stared at me with such a dreamy expression, my thoughts were momentarily jolted back to the night when, at the tender age of sixteen, I had met members of the Rolling Stones at the Phone Booth Club. Had I simpered over rock stars Keith Richards, Bill Wyman, and Brian Jones in the same manner that these ardent adolescents were fawning over me? When I came out of my reverie, I smiled at the crowd of boys that was still surrounding me.

"Would you sign one for me and my sister?"

"Hold on a minute! I was next!"

As I continued to scribble my name across their glossy publicity photos of my chick rock duo, they assured me that "Emily Muff is bound to be *very famous* one day!"

174

The group of pre-teen and adolescent males continued to loiter around me in the auditorium until I finished signing the last of their programs. Once this task was completed, I rewarded them with another smile, and announced that I needed to split because my manager was waiting backstage to tell me the news about a record deal. This produced a fresh outburst of ogling before these Emily Muff fans finally began to disperse. As I made my way to the post-gig party, I had an aching hand (and super-inflated ego!).

When I arrived backstage, I saw that the festivities were well under way. Members of Family were milling about with drinks in their hands, while several groupie chicks wearing low-cut mini-dresses flirted unabashedly with them. Janet spotted me, and rushed in my direction. "'Hey Moo! Where have you been?"

"Sorry for the delay, but . . . well . . . I was waylaid by a mob of Emily Muff fans, and I stopped to sign a bunch of autographs for them."

Janet's eyes widened in surprise. "You're kidding!" she exclaimed. I shook my head, and told her that I had searched for Lotus after the show. When I didn't find him backstage, I decided to check out the concert hall. Suddenly, this crowd of young guys came rushing in through one of the side doors, and had started begging me for my autograph. "Wow! So, how did it feel to be mobbed by the masses?" Em replied with a chuckle. I sauntered over to a nearby table, scooped up a plate with a piece of cake on it, and forked a glop of gooey frosting in my mouth.

"Piece of cake!" I quipped.

When I finally bumped into Lotus at the post-gig festivities several minutes later, he explained that scouts from Reprise Records had left immediately after the concert, and he would not find out the results of Emily Muff's audition until the following afternoon.

Janet and I arrived at Bradgate Bush the next day, eager to hear the news. Once we were seated in our manager's office, he informed us that Reprise had been impressed by Emily Muff's performance at De Montfort Hall—and a deal with this record label was in the offing.

"Oh, that's so fantastic!" I exclaimed.

"Woah, Baby! Just show me the dotted line!" Em chimed in. She was grinning so broadly, her smile seemed to stretch across her face. Our whoops of glee continued for another minute, making it virtually impossible for Tony to get another word in edgewise. Once our cheering had finally subsided, our manager offered us his congratulations. He then went on to say that he'd already booked Emily Muff into Olympic Sound Studios to record a demo single. Engineer George Chkiantz, who had worked on albums for Led Zeppelin and Soft Machine, was to be at the helm of the mixing-board that evening.

"Wow! That's great new, Lotus!" Janet exclaimed.

"Yeah, Olympic is one of the top studios around, isn't it?" I chimed in.

Tony nodded and strutted around the room for a bit. Then he turned towards the two of us and his face took on a more serious expression. "Now remember, girls, Emily Muff might not have received a record deal without my help."

Chapter Thirty-Three

"My Way" Or the Highway

Emily Muff had played a series of gigs at London's Klooks Kleek venue, and concerts in both Plymouth and Southampton. We also appeared with Family at the Lyceum in London. The rock groups Steppenwolf and Van der Graaf Generator had also been booked on the same bill. These big-name bands obviously weren't soft rock groups . . . and neither was our chick rock duo. We loved performing our songs that featured bar chords, lead guitar, soaring harmonies, quirky keyboard arpeggios, and rockin' harmonica solos.

Our duo was so busy, in fact, that there had been no time to meet with our manager before the night that Emily Muff was to record its demo tape. When Janet and I arrived at Olympic Sound Studios for the session, members of Family greeted us in the control room. After Em and I set our Telecasters down, our Lots Road buddies introduced us to engineer George Chkiantz. We conversed with this recording wizard for several minutes, and then began removing our electric guitars from their hard-shell cases.

"Umm . . . would you hold on a second, girls!" one of the Leicester Lads called out. "Didn't Tony tell you that Family has already laid down the instrumentation for the song 'My Way' that we've written for your session tonight?" Janet and I set our instruments back in their protective containers, and stared at him in disbelief.

Whaaat? Not record an Emily Muff original?

To make matters worse, we knew that Frank Sinatra had already released a song with the same name the previous March. Considering the title, it seemed ironic that our duo was not being asked to showcase one of its songs at this recording session. "Obviously Em and I brought our Tele's to Olympic tonight because we were expecting to record an Emily Muff original," I replied. "How come you guys waited until *now* to make such a major announcement?" As I was speaking, our manager Tony arrived on the scene. It was clear from the strained expression on his face that he had quickly sussed the situation. He waved members of Family aside, and requested that the two of us speak with him in private. Em and I accompanied Lotus to one corner of the control room, where he attempted to placate us by explaining that various rock groups had not played on their demo record session, either. According to hearsay:

1) Guitarist Jimmy Page was a session musician on the Who's debut record.

2) The Beatles had not played instruments on their first album.

3) A dusty pile of tapes was stored in the vaults of Olympic Sound Studios that could substantiate this latter rumor.

Our manager went on to explain that the two of us would be singing vocals on the song. "Now hold on a friggin' minute!" Janet retorted. "Kathy and I thought we were going to be recording an Emily Muff original for our demo record. So, we brought our Tele's with us to the studio. Then we learn that Family's already written a song for this session, and has laid down the instrumental track. And now you're telling us that all we need to do is record vocals—for a song that we didn't even write?"

"Yeah, for crying out loud, Tony!" I chimed in. "If you think our songs suck, or that we're not competent musicians, then why did you invite us to tour with Family in the first place?" Lotus ignored our protests, and reminded us that the clock was ticking away. Olympic was one of the most expensive studios in London, and we were arguing to the tune of mega-money per minute. According to him, Reprise controlled the cash and his hands were metaphorically tied by the moguls of this record label.

I glanced across the room at guitarist Charlie to seek his support, but he seemed unwilling to meet my gaze. Family's vocalist, Roger, appeared to be studying some imaginary object on the floor. Even engineer George Chkiantz's composure looked like it had been ruffled; he was huddled over the mixing board, fiddling with the knobs on the console, and looking pissed-off that his precious engineering expertise was being wasted.

As the minutes continued to tick away, the deadlock between

Bradgate Bush and Emily Muff intensified. Tony kept reminding Em and me that it was imperative we trust the record company's judgment. The more Lotus argued with us, the more inflexible he seemed to become. By this time, it was obvious that Janet and I were seeing a side of our manager's personality that he had previously kept under wraps, and I found myself growing increasingly alarmed.

How could such a blatant breach of communication and trust have occurred between Bradgate Bush and Emily Muff?

If Family and Tony got their way, what guarantee did we have that it would ever be Emily Muff's way? I'd never dreamed that our rock duo would find itself embroiled in such an alarming stand-off with our manager so soon after its audition for Reprise. Why hadn't Em and I been told beforehand that we would not be recording an Emily Muff original at Olympic?

Janet motioned for me to step out into the hallway with her. As the two of us huddled outside the control room, we continued to feel stymied and in shock. Didn't these guys understand that the song they were asking our duo to record had *nothing* to do with Emily Muff's music? My bandmate thrust her hands on her hips and said that she couldn't believe we had no idea that Lotus and Family had been collaborating behind our backs like this. As she spoke, I realized with chagrin that perhaps this screw-up had been partly our fault. With hindsight, it was clear that we had failed to safeguard our interests by not keeping tabs on what Family and Reprise Records had planned for our band.

"Ugh! It's partly our fault, too," I replied. "Obviously, we should have made sure to clarify things with Lotus *before* we came into the studio tonight." Janet said that it was too late to be pointing out what we should have done. The two of us were at the studio now—and we needed to put on a united front. When our duo entered the control room, once again, I was further dismayed to hear that members of Family were engaged in a discussion about temperamental females.

By that point in time, it was obvious that Emily Muff had lost the battle of the vinyl. Family had already laid down the instrumental track for their song called "My Way," and suddenly they were requesting that I record a ('token?') woodwind part to add to the instrumental track. I finally ended up doing so, but only in an attempt to preserve the fragile peace.

After that, all that remained was for Em and me to record the vocals.

My friend and I held our emotions in check as we filed into the studio below, clutching lyric sheets for the Whitney/Chapman song "My Way." We then sat down on a pair of stools, positioned headphones over our ears, and leaned towards our respective microphones. While waiting for my auditory cue, I glanced over at Janet as she scanned the lyric sheet. Tension in the studio remained high, and I noticed that several veins were standing out along the sides of her neck.

"Are you ready, girls?" George Chkiantz was asking. We nodded in response, and the first notes of the instrumental track came barreling through the "cans." Em and I soon got the gist of the song, but it was so far removed from the ones that we wrote, it was tough for either of us to feel that it was representative of our duo's music. Finally, my bandmate flung off her headphones and yelled, "Stop the tape!"

"Cut!" the engineer responded. I heard the reel whoosh to a halt, and then the sound of it being rewound on its giant spools. I turned towards Janet. She was staring up at Tony in the control room.

"Look, you guys!" Em called out. "It's obvious that this session is going nowhere!" She went on to explain that it was difficult for her to relate to the song. I nodded, and said that it seemed like Emily Muff was being denied its artistic freedom. As I spoke, I could see Tony's rigid stance outlined in the semi-darkness of the control room upstairs. He leaned over the microphone at the mixing board, and his voice boomed over the intercom.

"Can you girls save your histrionics until *after* the recording session?" he barked. Janet and I glared back at him.

"This just isn't working!" Em countered. She slipped off her stool, and headed back up the stairs. I rose from my seat, as well. When I arrived in the control room, our manager was in a major huff, and members of Family were openly glaring at Janet and me. I suspected that our musician buddies had been shocked to learn that their preconceived notions regarding Emily Muff's recording session had been challenged by the two of us.

Even though Em and I knew that our rigorous stance was not going to help our track record with the moguls of the music business, our duo's principles were at stake.

And we were determined to stick to them.

So, we grabbed our Telecasters and hustled out of the building. As the two of us made our way down the front steps, I felt proud that our chick rock duo had not succumbed to Family's unfair demands . . . but I also couldn't help wondering about the fate of Emily Muff.

Chapter Thirty-Four

Double-Hitched

After the debacle at Olympic Sound Studios, an uneasy truce emerged between Bradgate Bush and Emily Muff. Even though the recording of our debut single had been put on hold, our duo was still booked to open shows, so we continued to hit the road with Family. After a concert at Fairfield Halls, Emily Muff had also been interviewed by a reporter from *The Croydon Press*.

As it happened, our duo was so busy touring that Tony had not yet informed us about *another* issue that had been brewing behind-the-scenes. Apparently, the British Home Office had contacted him, since Em and I were working in the UK, but still officially tourists. To keep out of any legal trouble, we had been popping over to the continent periodically, and then re-entering Great Britain with a fresh stamp on our passports that granted us additional months to remain there. By the time Lotus had heard from the Home Office, it was clear that our previous strategy was no longer going to work.

So, Tony arranged for us to consult with Family's solicitor, in the hope of finding a way for Em and me to become lawful residents of the UK. When the two of us arrived for our appointment, the Barrister had a frown on his face that was quite unsettling. He only exchanged a few pleasantries with us, and got right to the point by summarizing what I understood to be the following:

> Janet and I were in danger of being deported. There was only one option to lawfully remain in the UK and continue touring. Each of us must have a marriage of convenience with a British citizen. This would take place during an official ceremony at a Registrar's Office, where both couples would sign a legal Marriage Certificate for the British governmental paperwork.

The solicitor went on to add that what he was telling us must not, under any circumstances, be construed as legal advice.

Janet and I were stunned. We had obviously heard about so-called marriages of convenience. In fact, an American friend of ours had wed an Englishman who was an acquaintance of hers, and she'd been legally residing in the UK for over five years. Still, Em and I never dreamed that we would be personally forced to take such drastic measures. In the end, this same friend of ours offered to help us out. Her "hubby" happened to know two British blokes named Allan and Dave, who just might be hip to Emily Muff's predicament. It turned out that they were. Less than a week later, she informed us that both Allan and Dave had volunteered to help us out, with no strings attached.

Although it was weird waiting for two strangers to telephone and "propose" to Em and me, that's exactly what happened. Then, on a blustery day in mid-February, Paddy drove Emily Muff in his Rolls to the Kensington and Chelsea Register Office, where I was to "marry" Allan—and Janet was to "tie the knot" with Dave. It was a double wedding, and a blur in my mind. The only thing I remember was turning my face away from Allan when the Registrar said, "You may now kiss your bride."

It was a bizarre wedding ceremony, indeed.

Afterwards, the four of us signed the paperwork. As we walked out of the building, a wedding photographer (paid by Reprise, of course) was waiting. Tony gathered both couples around him and insisted that publicity photos be taken, with him in the middle.

"Come on everybody! Smile!" our manager bellowed. "It's your fucking wedding day!"

Chapter Thirty-Five

The Record Executive

Around the same time as Emily Muff's double wedding, the band Traffic was re-forming, and Simon and Garfunkel had officially disbanded. Guitarist Eric Clapton was busy touring in the States with Delaney and Bonnie, and Sandy Denny was forming a group called Fotheringay with her husband Trevor Lucas. Janet and I were especially pleased to hear the news that producer Mickie Most had signed a female bassist named Suzi Quatro to his RAK label.

Although Em and I agreed that our double-wedding had been a dire solution to our duo's dilemma, we were now legally permitted to work in the UK. So, in addition to being billed to open shows with the Leicester Lads, Emily Muff made an appearance with Family on BBC London-TV, singing backup for their new single, "Today." Next, our manager informed us that an executive at Reprise Records had requested that we meet with him to discuss a recording contract with his record label.

It was difficult to keep my excitement under wraps as Lotus escorted Janet and me into the posh offices of Reprise Records. Our duo had worked so hard for this moment! We were proud of our accomplishments, and counting on our meeting with the record executive to go smoothly. Once the three of us arrived at the reception desk, our manager stated the nature of our business. The woman seated there motioned for us to follow her into the inner sanctum of Reprise. As we walked past a series of partitioned cubicles, I noticed that the walls were lined with elaborately-framed album covers depicting the various artists represented by this prestigious company. Several employees glanced up from their desks, and openly gaped at our mini-procession as it headed towards the VIP wing. By the expression on their faces, it was obvious that Emily Muff was the First Female Rock Duo in Britain to be negotiating a recording contract with this mega-record label.

The receptionist stopped outside the executive's office, and motioned for us to wait in the hallway. I watched as she opened the door, and shimmied deftly into his domain. While waiting, we chatted with Tony about the meeting we were about to walk into, even teasing him that he might be nervous, too. That's when Lotus said he wouldn't be accompanying us in there.

"What? How come you're not going in with us?" I asked him point-blank. Our manager skillfully evaded the question, and tried to placate us with a pep-talk, instead. Although he soon realized that this tactic was fizzling with Em and me, Lotus remained adamant that he would not be attending the meeting. Instead, he promised to rendezvous with us in the reception area once we had our recording contract in hand. Our manager's behavior was bewildering, but before we had a chance to question him further, the receptionist reappeared and announced that Emily Muff's interview would commence shortly. Upon hearing the news, Tony gave the two of us a thumbs-up sign and promptly departed with the Reprise employee back in the direction of the lobby.

Once they had disappeared from view, I whispered in Janet's ear, "What's up with Lotus?" My bandmate shrugged her shoulders and frowned.

"Who knows, Moo . . . ? But I can't believe he's deserting our band again!" She went on to say that maybe Tony had chickened out at the last minute. Ordinarily her remark might have elicited a chuckle from us both, but the fact remained that we were standing in a hallway, on our own, once again. Several more minutes passed. We continued to wait anxiously in the corridor outside the record executive's office, wondering whether he was occupied with an urgent matter—or purposely building up the suspense as a business ploy. Whatever the case, it felt like an eternity before the door finally opened and a tall, slender man appeared on the threshold.

After brief introductions were made, the record executive invited us into his stately office. He then motioned towards a pair of chairs that were facing his desk. Once the three of us were seated, he explained that his record company had been carefully tracking Emily Muff's musical career. According to him, officials at Reprise loved our duo's sound, and the company was prepared to sign a recording contract with us.

"That's wonderful!" I blurted out.

Janet nodded. "We know how many terrific bands your company represents, and our duo appreciates the opportunity to be on your label." As she spoke, the businessman began toying around with an official-looking document on his desk. I leaned forward in my chair, and tried to get a glimpse of the particulars. Didn't he understand that the suspense for fledgling recording artists was excruciating? Finally, the music mogul smiled, and told us again that his company loved our music. He then paused, licked his lips suggestively, and asked the two of us what we would do for *him*.

I was in such a state of raw anticipation, it took me several seconds longer than it should have to realize that this big cheese at Reprise was no longer making references as to how much his company admired Emily Muff's music. My mind flashed on images of groupies performing a variety of sex acts for Tony and members of Family. Was that what this record exec wanted from us? Although Janet and I had been eager to nab a record deal in the bud, it seemed as though he had anticipated having a private nip at Emily Muff's "bud" before we signed on the dotted line. Surely this top-level record executive wouldn't stoop so low as to request sexual favors from our duo.

Or would he?

As the seconds ticked away, the businessman's sleazy demeanor continued to reek of the notorious "casting-couch" scenario, and I cringed in shock at this unexpected turn of events. How dare he imply that we should suck him (or fuck him?) in return for a record deal!

"WHAT did you say?" I retorted.

The record company official glared at me, and then rose from his chair. As he did so, I half-expected another part of his anatomy to be on the rise, as well. I kept my eyes fixated upon his face and studied the lecherous glint that still seemed to be reflected in his eyes. It was clear that this guy had dropped all pretense of a professional business demeanor. Was he about to do the same with his trousers?

By then, my initial shock and disbelief had turned to anger. I tilted my chin upwards and was about to deliver a scathing verbal rebuttal, but Janet beat me to the punch. She jumped out of her chair, and thrust her middle finger at him. I sprang up from my seat as well. And with that, Emily Muff stormed out of the record executive's office.

Chapter Thirty-Six

Standing Our Ground

When Em and I arrived back in the lobby, Tony intercepted us near the reception desk. "How'd the meeting go, girls?" he wanted to know. Neither Janet nor I replied. We were too busy wondering whether any other band in the history of rock 'n' roll had ever dared to challenge a top honcho at the London offices of Reprise Records. Probably not, as most musicians were beating down the door in the opposite direction.

Em and I hurried out of the building in a flurry of fury and disgust. We did not say a word to anyone, including Lotus, who followed closely behind with his eyebrows furrowed. Once the three of us were outside, I drew in several deep gulps of air, not knowing whether to laugh, cry, vomit, or scream. My hands were shaking so much, I was forced to grip the nearest parking meter for support. How could Emily Muff's record deal with Reprise have gone sleazy-kaput in a matter of minutes? I glanced back at the building which housed the offices of this prestigious record label, and noticed that it was located at number *sixty-nine* New Oxford Street. I pointed in the direction of these decorative numerals, and let out a derisive snort.

"Hey, Em! You see that? We should have known how things would turn out today when we saw the record company's friggin' address." Her eyes followed my gaze, and our laughter bordered on the hysterical as it echoed down the street. Then we turned back towards our manager and began describing in detail what had happened during the meeting. Tony shook his head and insisted that we must have misunderstood what the record executive was saying.

"There's no way we could have misunderstood him," I insisted. "It was obvious that he had something sexual in mind, like a blow job." Janet folded her arms in front of her, and told Lotus we weren't about to put up with that kind of crap in exchange for a recording contract. My bandmate continued by saying that the executive's behavior had been so sleazy, she had given him the finger.

"You did WHAT?" Tony bellowed.

"Look! We're just not into that whole 'casting-couch' scenario," I snapped back.

Several passersby stopped to stare at the altercation that was taking place between the three of us outside the offices of Reprise. Lotus squared his shoulders and continued to insist that Em and I had misinterpreted the record executive's motives. As I listened to our manager's rationale, I wondered why he wasn't siding with us.

"Now wait a minute, Lotus," Janet interjected. "Don't you believe what we're telling you?" She went on to suggest that the record executive might have expected to get away with his lewd request, simply because he saw us as a couple of chicks desperate to sign with his record label. Our manager shook his head again. Although he seemed to become more exasperated by the minute, my friend and I were adamant about standing our ground. After all, we were the ones who had been present at the meeting.

"Oh, come on, Tony!" I exclaimed. "Can't you understand that Em and I would rather blow a recording contract than give some big-wig a blow job?" Janet nodded her head.

"Yeah! If you'd been present at our meeting with him, all this crap wouldn't have happened in the first place," she pointed out.

Lotus abruptly turned away from the two of us, and began hurrying down New Oxford Street. As we watched his retreating form, I felt a mixture of anger and frustration. After all, Janet and I had already forfeited what was supposed to have been a fabulous recording contract with Reprise.

Would we lose our manager, as well?

When my bandmate and I caught up with Tony at the end of the block, the tension between the three of us remained so tight it resembled a time-bomb about to explode. The traffic light flashed an emerald green, and our manager resumed walking at a fast-paced clip. He kept this up for a while, but finally slowed his steps. Then he swiveled around, and darted a series of dagger-like glances in our direction. Despite his ultra-frosty demeanor, it was important to me that Lotus understand our point of view. So, I called out to him. "Won't you listen a minute, Tony?" He did not reply, and I took the opportunity to continue. "Janet and I obviously want our duo to succeed, but we refuse to compromise our principles, you dig?"

"All I know is that you girls have really gone and screwed things up this time."

"But that's precisely what we *didn't* do!" Em defended our duo. The two of us continued to stare at our manager in disbelief. Why was it so difficult for him to understand that we refused to trade sexual favors for a recording contract? Tony thrust his hands into his trouser pockets.

"I'm bloody well pissed off at you both! Family has gone out of their way to invite your duo to tour with them. And don't forget that I was the one who brought Emily Muff to the attention of Reprise in the first place!" He scrunched his eyes tightly closed for a moment, before opening them slowly. Next, he ran his fingers through his hair, and sighed.

"Well, if *you* don't believe what happened back at Reprise today, then nobody will!" I exclaimed. My voice was cracking. I clamped my mouth shut and hoped the tears that were threatening to cascade down my cheeks would miraculously remain in check. As the three of us continued arguing, the traffic whizzed by at an alarming rate of speed. Horns blared and the stench from exhaust fumes filled my nostrils. By then, our manager was also insisting that Janet and I had treated the record executive rudely and unprofessionally.

According to Lotus, the record deal had been an amazing opportunity, and it was all our fault that we'd thrown it away. Janet and I had thought that securing a lucrative contract with Reprise would be a dream-come-true, as well . . . but not after we had witnessed the record executive's sordid demands that day. We glanced at each other, knowing that it was pointless for us to try and reason with our manager any longer.

In the meantime, a deep, guttural moan was rising from the back of Tony's throat. It seemed as if the other shoe might drop at any second, and I cringed. "I know how close you've been with Family, girls, but this arrangement just doesn't seem to be working out," he announced.

"Oh, that's just terrific, Lotus!" Janet retorted. "I've been waiting for you to get to the part where you tell us that Bradgate Bush is going to dump our duo!"

"Yeah! Thanks a lot!" I sneered. "In spite of everything, we really do appreciate that *you* never asked us for a blow job." The sarcasm in my voice dripped from my tongue like melting ice. I glanced at Lotus with one final, soul-searching gaze, but his face had become a mask of impassivity. How could we have been so naïve to think that our manager would be immune to the lure of mega-money when it came to a recording contract for Emily Muff? It was obvious that the cocoon-like safety net that Janet and I had expected Bradgate Bush to provide had merely been a figment of our imagination.

"Come on, Moo! Let's get out of here," my bandmate said. The two of us were silent as we turned away from the man we had (erroneously) assumed would be Emily Muff's Rock of Gibraltar in the British music scene. As we headed towards the Tottenham Court Road Tube station, it felt as though my body had been sliced to the core.

Would we ever secure representation with a company that would be hip to our duo's principles, as well as its music?

Chapter Thirty-Seven

The Strength Within

Our disconcerting experience at Reprise was not the first time that Em and I had been confronted by a shocking, unexpected turn of events. After returning home that afternoon, we were more resolved than ever to overcome obstacles like these, if and when they arose in the future.

After all, we had already weathered unforeseen roadblocks such as:

A sleazy stage door bouncer.

No dressing room for females.

Cat-calls from the crowd.

A disrespectful recording session.

And not being taken for our word.

Janet and I were no longer as naïve. We were determined to stand up for our principles again—and again, if necessary. After all, we were two courageous female musicians, blazing a trail through the labyrinth of the male-dominated British rock music scene. It was a task not for the faint of heart, one that required an iron will, tenacity, and a belief in ourselves, and our music.

As long as we never compromised our values and continued to follow our convictions, we would stay true to who we are—and what we envisioned for our chick rock duo.

Chapter Thirty-Eight

From Chrysalis to Butterfly

In refusing to compromise itself, Great Britain's First Female Rock Duo had retained its dignity, but at a hefty price. We had been left without a manager or a recording contract, and had also forfeited the chance to continue touring with the band Family. The myth of the "casting-couch" scenario had become a rock-solid reality in our lives and, for the next several days, we remained in a state of delusion and shock.

"You know," I confided to Janet one evening, "There are moments when I wish our duo could hop into some sort of time machine and be magically transported into the future, when there's bound to be more chick rock musicians in the music scene. Just think of it, Em!" I continued. "Wouldn't it be great for rockers like us to have the freedom to expend all of their energy creating amazing music— instead of having to deal with the type of harassment and hype that we've run into?"

"Well, things are bound to get better for female rock musicians in the future . . . simply because they can't get any worse!" Janet replied with a half-hearted chuckle. She walked over to me, and we gave each other a hug. "No matter how tough things have been for Emily Muff, we can't give up now! Think of all we've accomplished, Moo! Let's keep moving FORWARD!"

During the next several weeks, our duo moved forward in the literal sense when we rented an inexpensive, two-bedroom flat on Rosslyn Hill Road in London. In what seemed like an ironic twist of fate, our new digs had been vacated by record producer Ian Samwell, who we'd met previously through our DJ friend, Jeff Dexter. Although it was tempting to approach Ian regarding a possible business alliance, he was a producer for Warner Brothers Records. We had heard that Reprise was a subsidiary of this corporation, and felt that Ian might have an allegiance to both record companies. In lieu of this, I suggested that we contact the Incredible String Band's manager, Joe Boyd, who had previously expressed an interest in representing our duo. However, Em and I ended up ruling out this possibility, as well, because the majority of acts he produced and managed seem to be jazz, blues, or folk-oriented, and our chick rock duo was different. Finally, after much discussion, Janet suggested that Emily Muff take a chance on Chrysalis Records, since its label had signed a variety of rock bands. I agreed that we should give this company a try and, soon, our duo had secured an appointment with executives from this firm at their offices on Oxford Street.

On the day of our scheduled meeting at Chrysalis, we noticed that the less-than-elaborate décor in the lobby seemed in stark contrast to the furnishings at Reprise. However, Janet and I were pleased to see that the receptionist seated there had a friendly smile as we approached her desk. "You must be Emily Muff," she said, before escorting us into an office where a dark-haired businessman sat behind a desk. After introductions were made, the receptionist left the room, and the record executive motioned for the two of us to have a seat. We smiled at him, and then Janet explained about the instruments we played and that we wrote our own songs. She then went on to give the Chrysalis executive an overview of Emily Muff's rock 'n' roll resume. As she was speaking, a second businessman entered the office and sat down in a chair.

The music mogul seated behind the desk told us that he was aware of our duo's accomplishments. He paused, and then asked whether we had heard the rumor about our duo that was going around the industry. "What rumor?" I asked. The businessman explained that there was a rumor that Emily Muff had been turned down by Reprise records. I shook my head and said, "No, it was Emily Muff who rejected Reprise. Not the other way around!" He ignored my remark, and told us that, once a band was turned down by a major label, it was difficult for other record companies to consider that group to be a viable, highly-commercial commodity.

Janet and I knew that the rumor circulating was false. We were also aware that many managers and record companies relied on hype to pitch a band's image. I explained to these Chrysalis music moguls that our female duo had no wish to be a highly-commercial commodity that was hyped as some sort of rock 'n' roll anomaly. This was clearly not what these record executives had expected to hear, and an uncomfortable silence ensued. I glanced around the room. There were papers scattered on the desk, and several record albums were laying on the floor. As I transferred my attention back to the meeting at hand, both businessmen were rising from their seats. It was obvious that Emily Muff's interview with their record company was at an end.

I cleared my throat and said, "Before we leave, I'm curious. Just for the *record*, did you agree to meet with us today solely to satisfy your curiosity about the so-called Reprise rejects?" No response. Janet and I exited the building, and headed towards the nearest Tube station. "If those cats at Chrysalis had already decided not to sign our duo because of that rumor . . . then why did they meet with us in the first place?" I huffed.

"Ugh! The way things have been going, I'm surprised that some record executive hasn't suggested we change our duo's name to Emily Fluff!" my bandmate growled.

Chapter Thirty-Nine

Voices Like Crystal

One advantage of our duo's new-found freedom was the opportunity it gave Janet and me to be even more selective in choosing the direction that Emily Muff would take. So, we jumped at the chance to get back in the swing of things when Martin Stone and his band Mighty Baby invited us to add backup vocals on an album they were recording. When we arrived at Olympic Sound Studios on the night of the session, Feather Man and his buddies had already set up their gear. After greeting Janet and me, they introduced us to producer/sound engineer Glyn Johns, who had masterminded recordings for rock groups such as the Rolling Stones and Led Zeppelin.

Mighty Baby had already finished laying down the preliminary track for their song "Winter Passes," and they were requesting that Janet and I add backup vocals to it. Martin handed us the lyric sheet, and suggested that we do a couple of practice takes first. So, my bandmate and I filed into the studio. After donning a pair of headphones, we stepped up to the microphones, and began to sing along with the track. It felt great to be back in a studio setting, and it only took a couple of practice rounds before we got the gist of the song. Glyn Johns seemed pleased with our efforts, as well, and suggested that we do a take. Once we returned to the control room, Martin and his musician buddies complimented us on the vocals that we had added. They also requested that our duo hang around the studio in case they wanted us to record some additional backup vocals later in the session.

While everyone listened to the playback of "Winter Passes," Em and I sat down cross-legged on the floor in a corner of the control room, while the engineer Glyn Johns and Mighty Baby conferred about the mix. Suddenly, their conversation was interrupted by the sound of voices emanating over the intercom systems that connected the studios.

"Man! I dig those chick vocals!" some guy was saying.

"Yeah! Their voices sound like crystal, don't they, Mick?"

Although their words were a bit muffled, it was obvious that a man named Mick had been eavesdropping on Mighty Baby's recording session from another studio in the building. Engineer Glyn Johns jacked up the volume on the intercom, and we listened some more. Soon, there could be little doubt that it had been members of the Rolling Stones who were discussing the vocal merits of Emily Muff. Glyn Johns turned towards Janet and me, and said that it sounded as though Mick and Keith liked our voices. I was stoked to hear that these rock stars thought our voices sounded like crystal, and it was difficult to refrain from whooping with glee. Martin and his bandmates seemed happy for us, but I wondered if they were feeling a bit put-out by the special attention Emily Muff had received.

In the meantime, Glyn Johns had flipped off the intercom switch and returned to the task of engineering Mighty Baby's session. Although my bandmate and I remained outwardly composed, knowing that Mick and Keith were in a studio nearby made me want to slink over to the intercom, switch it back on, and eavesdrop on their recording session. At the same time, I knew that Martin and his band might want us to record additional vocals for them, so I kept my fanny rooted firmly to the floor.

Several minutes later, the door to the control room opened. The recording session came to a halt, once again, as the young man standing there walked over to the mixing board. I watched as he began speaking with Glyn Johns and Feather Man's band. As they continued to chat together, the stranger swiveled around several times, and pointed at Janet and me. Although we could not make out what was being said, my friend and I were curious as to what was up. Less than a minute later, someone from Mighty Baby called out to Em and me. "Mick and Keith have invited you girls into their recording session."

Wow! An invitation for Emily Muff to check out a Rolling Stones recording session!

I turned towards Janet. Her eyes had opened wide, like mine, yet we both somehow managed to keep our cool. I glanced over at the mixing board. All of the guys gathered there were staring at my bandmate and me as they waited for us to respond to the mind-blowing invitation from Mick and Keith.

Although it was obvious that mingling with the Glimmer Twins might propel our duo's career into the stratosphere, Janet and I knew that each and every move we made was crucial. After all:

Emily Muff was the First Female Rock Duo in Britain.

A trailblazing role that had far-reaching influence.

Our band's reputation was clearly on the line. It had the potential to affect not only our duo, but the status of chick rockers in the future.

It was tempting to accept Mick and Keith's enticing invitation, yet Em and I also understood the importance of keeping our word to our Lots Road buddies. After all, we had promised to be on hand at their recording session in case they needed us to add more backup vocals. Janet and I leaned towards each other and, with imperceptible shakes of our heads, wordlessly communicated our decision to remain at Mighty Baby's session. I turned towards the guy who had delivered the message from Mick and Keith and called out to him.

"Thanks, but Janet and I have promised to stay here and record some more vocals for Mighty Baby's session tonight." The messenger from the Rolling Stones glowered at the two of us, and then he hustled out of the control room. Once he had left, Martin and his bandmates seemed to breathe a collective sigh of relief, and they flashed the two of us a series of grateful smiles.

Chapter Forty

The Glimmer Twins

Mighty Baby's recording session resumed shortly, and Janet and I began chatting together in hushed tones. Suddenly she stopped in mid-sentence and her eyes opened wide, once again. "Don't look now . . . but Mick and Keith are standing in the doorway!"

What? The Glimmer Twins?

I glanced around discreetly, and saw that Mick and Keith were loitering in the entranceway of Mighty Baby's studio. They were boldly staring at my bandmate and me—and then these megastars stepped into the room. Em and I watched as the two of them sauntered over to the mixing board. Soon, they were engaged in a discussion with Glyn Johns and members of Mighty Baby. As they conferred together, Mick and Keith kept swiveling around and eyeballing Janet and me. By then, it was clear that the conversation was centered around Emily Muff.

After another minute or so, Feather Man turned towards us. "Mick and Keith want to know if you chicks would like to check out their recording session," he announced. As he spoke, a hush swept over the room. Em and I glanced at each other in an effort to compose ourselves. After all, it was one thing to reject the messenger that the Glimmer Twins had sent in earlier. But quite another to turn down Mick and Keith in person!

As the silence in the room continued, I found myself wondering whether:

1) These rock stars wanted us to provide Hohner harp or backup vocals for their session.

2) They had something more *intimate* in mind.

A rush of intense, mixed emotions coursed through me. Should Emily Muff sashay away with Mick and Keith into their studio? Or remain at Mighty Baby's recording session, as we had promised? We knew that deserting Martin and his buddies would be tantamount to a betrayal of their trust, yet the two of us hesitated as we continued to ponder our dilemma.

The Glimmer Twins must have been wondering why we were taking so long to decide, and members of Mighty Baby seemed curious, as well. However, Em and I knew that our duo's reputation was at stake. So, Janet finally called out to these two megastars, "We appreciate the offer, but Kathy and I have promised to record some other vocals for Mighty Baby's session tonight." Mick and Keith stared at us in seeming disbelief. After all, who in their right minds turned down an invitation from the Rolling Stones?

Once it was clear that Emily Muff's final decision had been made, I raised my hand in thanks to these rock stars, but the Glimmer Twins remained silent as they made their way towards the exit. "I hope they won't think of Em and me as a couple of ungrateful, snooty chicks," I thought to myself. When Mick and Keith had disappeared from view, I felt a heart-wrenching, sinking feeling. Had Emily Muff just made the most monumental mistake of its career?

In the meantime, Glyn Johns had turned his attention back to the mixing board. Martin and the other members of Mighty Baby smiled at Janet and me. It was clear that they were pleased that Emily Muff had not succumbed to the lure of the Rolling Stones. Mighty Baby's recording session soon resumed an air of normalcy. However, visions of Mick and Keith continued to dance across my mind, and I found myself second-guessing our duo's decision. Had any other bands in the history of rock 'n' roll been daring (or foolish?) enough to reject an offer to hang out at a Rolling Stones session?

Later that night, after Mighty Baby had wrapped up at Olympic, Martin and his buddies dropped Em and me off at our flat. We thanked them for the lift, and the opportunity to record backup vocals for their album. After Feather Man and his bandmates had driven away, I unlocked our front door and the two of us stepped inside. As we headed up the staircase, I continued to think about Mick and Keith, and their foray into Mighty Baby's recording session. Janet must have been thinking about them, too.

"I know it was a tough decision, Moo," she began. "First, Mick and

Keith eavesdrop on our vocals—and *then* they invite us into their recording session. That's a pretty heavy trip, isn't it?"

"You're damn right it is!" I answered. The two of us entered our flat, closed the door behind us and set our bags down on the kitchen table.

"Well, we really didn't know what Mick and Keith wanted from us anyway," Em remarked. I nodded and said that it seemed like we'd made the right decision by keeping our promise to Mighty Baby. The two of us were silent for a moment, and then a sheepish grin began spreading across my face.

"But I have to confess that I'm still feeling some pangs of regret that we gave up the opportunity to check out Mick and Keith's recording session . . ."

"Check out their session, my ass!" Em snickered. "Don't give me that bull! You wanted to check out a lot more than Keith's guitar riffs! Just how were you planning to resist his rock star allure, eh?"

Chapter Forty-One

Skip to My Lew

Not long afterwards, Janet and I heard that an American manager/producer named Lew had arrived in London from New York. He was looking for bands to sign with him and, once my friend and I found out his contact information, we telephoned the hotel where he was staying. After giving the businessman a verbal run-down on Emily Muff, he agreed to audition us the following day. I was pleased that Lew seemed genuinely interested in our duo, but felt a bit wary that he had suggested we bring our instruments to his London lodgings. "I wonder why he's holding the audition at his hotel, rather than a rehearsal studio." I remarked to Janet later that evening.

"Would you cool it, Moo!" she replied. "I know we had a lousy experience with both Chrysalis and Reprise, but let's give this guy a break, okay? Besides, I think he mentioned something about his wife and kids being here in London with him."

When we arrived at Lew's hotel the next day, a man of medium build with dark hair and a friendly smile intercepted us in the lobby. Once introductions had been made, he led us into his hotel suite. Janet and I set our instruments down and, less than a minute later, a brunette woman with several young children in tow appeared in the doorway of the adjoining room. Lew introduced us to his family, and said that they would be sequestered next door during Emily Muff's audition. Once his wife and kids had left the room, the businessman motioned for Janet and me to unpack our gear. We popped open our guitar cases and took out Emily Muff's Telecasters. After plugging them into Lew's portable amp, I slipped my flute and Hohner harmonicas from their cases. As we finished setting up, Lew sat down opposite Em and me in a lavishly-upholstered armchair. He then asked us whether we had ever considered expanding our line-up to include a rhythm section.

"Well, the idea's crossed our minds," I explained, "But to be honest, I think we'd rather remain a duo." Then I half-jokingly asked whether he was expecting Emily Muff to find additional musicians and morph into a five-piece chick rock band.

"It's a thought," Lew replied with a grin. Janet took a deep breath, and sighed. She explained that, even if we wanted to add a female rhythm section, we hadn't heard of many chick rockers playing bass or drums in London.

"We know that Maureen Tucker plays drums with the Velvet Underground in the States. Bassist Suzie Quatro is here in London, but she's already spoken for," I interjected. Lew leaned back in his chair and told us that he would have our best interests at heart, should he decide to sign us. As I listened to his words, they sounded a bit vague . . . and perhaps a little too good to be true. After all, it wasn't the first time that Emily Muff had been given a similar line, and I felt the need to question him further.

"Excuse me," I began. "Could you be more specific about what you mean by having our best interests at heart? You see, it's important that we have a manager who's willing to allow us artistic freedom. We obviously want our duo to make it big, but feel that chick musicians should be respected on the basis of the music they play."

Although it appeared as though Lew had been listening to me, I wasn't sure that he necessarily agreed with what I was saying. As our meeting with him continued, he let us know that he felt our female lineup was a rarity in the rock 'n' roll scene, an undeniable selling point. Em and I knew that our trailblazing duo was, indeed, unusual in the world of British rock. Yet Lew seemed to have his own, preconceived notions about Emily Muff. He requested that we lighten up a bit, and enjoy capitalizing on the uniqueness of our group's female make-up. As he spoke, I found myself wondering, "How can this guy be making such crucial decisions about our duo . . . before he's even heard us play a single note?" The thought of this made me feel uncomfortable, and I figured that Janet must be inwardly cringing, too. However, we both knew that we needed to secure new management for our duo. So, Em and I continued to talk shop with him.

Finally, Lew requested that we play him a medley of Emily Muff originals, and we began with our song "Time Does Fly."

"Winter brings a biting wind,
To the street where you've gone to meet him.
Haunted thoughts are coming fast,
A year has passed you by . . .
Since you've seen him,
Time does fly.
So many changes you've been through,
Trying to forget him.
How many records have you listened to?
Still the same old song . . ."

It was important to Em and me that we showcase an array of instruments and a wide range of vocal harmonies. So, we also included in our audition excerpts from our songs, "Return and Beyond," "Country Air," and our two-guitar instrumental "Essence." As we were playing, Lew leaned forward in his chair with a look of concentration on his face. Once Janet and I had finished our mini-set, he rose from his seat and sprinted into the adjoining room. Moments later, he returned with his wife and children and requested that we repeat our songs for his spouse to hear.

Emily Muff performed several numbers for her, but one of the children knocked an ashtray off the coffee table, burst into tears, and promptly put an end to our audition. We set our instruments down while Lew reached over and hoisted his wailing son onto his lap. His wife smiled at Janet and me and said that she had enjoyed hearing our duo's unique sound. It seemed as though she was about to say something else, but another one of their children began to cry. Lew's wife hastily gathered her brood together, and they disappeared into the adjoining room. Once a semblance of order had returned to the audition area, the businessman informed us that he had been impressed with our music. He went on to say that he was eager to discuss the details of a contract with us, but was scheduled to fly back to New York the following day. Lew outlined his itinerary for the coming month, and explained that his company would draw up a written contract. Then, after returning to London, he would discuss the particulars of the deal with us. The businessman leaned back in his chair, and instructed the two of us to use the time that he was away to begin searching for a rhythm section to incorporate into Emily Muff.

"WHAT?" Janet exclaimed. "Add more musicians?"

"We've already told you how we feel about that . . . ," I chimed in. As I spoke, my bandmate nodded her head.

"Yeah, Kathy and I were under the impression that you were okay with Emily Muff being a duo, since you agreed to meet with us today." Lew shook his head and explained that, although our music had a unique quality, he felt it would be in our duo's best interest to create a fuller sound by adding a rhythm section. Listening to him speak, I began to feel a sinking feeling in the pit of my stomach. After all, if this guy had truly grooved on our duo's sound, why was he insisting that Emily Muff augment its line-up?

"Now wait a minute!" I began. "If Janet and I agree to sign with you, we need to know that you're not going to ask us to change anything else." Lew assured us that there was nothing else he wanted to alter. He then wrote out a check for our living expenses and studio rehearsal fees—and said he'd be in touch. Janet and I packed up our instruments, and the three of us shook hands. Although it was obvious that our duo had passed its audition with "flying" Fenders, I couldn't quite shake the nagging doubt at the back of my mind that Lew had not fully described just how he was planning to cash in on "Emily's Muff."

Once Janet and I returned home after the audition, I continued to wonder what was going to become of our chick rock duo now that Lew had entered the picture. After all, we had known him for less than twenty-four hours, and he was already demanding that we add a rhythm section. Although my bandmate and I had not signed a formal contract with Lew, our acceptance of his financial assistance during this interim period gave him a measure of control over the proverbial purse strings—and the management of Emily Muff.

Chapter Forty-Two

Recollections of Rob

After dinner that evening, Janet and I sat at the table in our kitchen and began discussing our audition for Lew earlier in the day. I mentioned that I'd felt a bit bummed out when he insisted that we add bass and drums to our lineup. Janet nodded, and said "Yeah, especially since Lew raised the topic *before* we had even played him a single note."

"It seems as though he has a preconceived notion . . . a sort of tunnel-vision when it comes to our duo, doesn't it?" I muttered. The two of us were silent as I rose from my seat and made each of us a cup of jasmine tea. Once I returned to the table I mentioned that I preferred that Emily Muff remain a duo. However, I wasn't totally opposed to adding a rhythm section—especially after Family's drummer, Rob, had jammed with Emily Muff during one of its soundchecks.

"Yeah, his drumming was amazing!" Janet exclaimed. "He knew our music well, and the three of us sounded terrific playing together." Em went on to say that we would have hired Rob on the spot, had he been available. It was clear that my bandmate and I would be open to adding a fabulous drummer, especially one like Rob (or a bass player as stellar as Ric). I took several sips of my jasmine tea, and sighed.

"You know, I still remember all the details about that time Rob jammed with us." As I spoke, I noticed that Janet's eyes had moistened. Several minutes passed as we both recalled the time when Rob had snuck over to his Ludwig drum kit in the middle of an Emily Muff pre-gig soundcheck, and began jamming along with our duo. As the three of us played together, Em and I had not missed a beat—and neither had Rob. He was an amazing musician and he knew our songs well. In fact, his drumming had sounded *perfect* with our duo.

Once the three of us had finished our informal jam that night, Janet and I had teasingly asked Rob whether he'd like to join our band. It was wishful thinking on our part. After all, he was the drummer for Family, one of the hottest rock 'n' roll bands on the British touring circuit. Later, after Janet and I had returned to our hotel room, we chatted privately about how it had been a no-brainer that Rob's dynamite drumming had enhanced our duo's sound.

Several drivers honked their horns on the street outside Emily Muff's London flat, and I jerked out of my reverie. By then our cups of tea had grown cold. It was obvious that Janet and I were no longer touring with Rob. Instead, we had a new manager named Lew on the horizon, who was demanding that we add a rhythm section of our own.

"Speaking of Family, I find it interesting that Lotus never once asked our duo to add a rhythm section during the entire time he was our manager," my flat mate observed. I stretched my arms out wide and grinned at her.

"Well, that's because he obviously grooved on our sound, and was confident that we'd be successful as a duo."

"And so were all those male Emily Muff fans who mobbed you at De Montfort Hall!" Janet replied with a chuckle. Although the hour was late, my friend and I continued to chat in our cozy kitchen. It was clear that neither Lotus, Rob, nor Ric was still in the picture, and we needed to move on. "Maybe . . . just maybe . . . we can find the right rhythm section," I muttered.

It was a tall order. Our duo had high standards, especially after being booked on the same bill with rock bands like Family, Yes, Steppenwolf, the Move, Van der Graaf Generator, the Nice, and Mighty Baby. However, in searching for a rhythm section of our own, Em and I knew that we needed to be realistic as well. So, we lowered our expectations (a tad) and agreed to begin our search for a drummer and bassist as Lew had requested.

Chapter Forty-Three

Fiddlin' Around

Prior to leaving for New York, Lew had booked Emily Muff in advance at the Country Club in London for its debut gig as a refurbished band. With this in mind, Janet and I asked our musician friends if they knew of any bass players or drummers who were between bands—and open to touring with two rocker chicks. It turned out that all of their chums already had working gigs, and we were momentarily back to square one.

In the meantime, Em and I jammed with several of our musician buddies in order to get the feel of a fuller sound. Next, we placed an ad for a rhythm section in the music publication *Melody Maker*. After receiving zero responses, we had to admit that maybe the (mostly) male rockers in London who were available to audition might not wish to join a female duo with the name Emily Muff. Still, we went ahead and placed another ad for both a bassist and drummer with the date that we would be holding open auditions at Studio 51 in London.

When that day rolled around, Janet and I entered the club and headed towards the stage with our Telecasters in hand. As we began unpacking our gear, Em suddenly had a faraway look in her eyes. "The last time we came here, I think we saw John Mayall jam with Tony McPhee," she mused.

"Yeah, I loved attending those weekly jam sessions," I replied. "And now we're back here again auditioning musicians for our *own* band!" The two of us grinned at each other, and resumed setting up for our open audition. We were so preoccupied with this task that neither of us noticed the slender guy with longish, ash-blonde hair standing in the doorway. As soon as he stepped further into the room, we both became aware of his presence. The young man had a friendly smile, and a violin case in his hand.

Although Emily Muff had not advertised for a violinist, I found myself curious to hear him play. Janet must have been intrigued by him, as well. She flashed the new arrival a welcoming smile, and then introduced the two of us. Em and I waited as he approached the stage. He told us his name was Steve, and inquired as to the whereabouts of the other members in our band. "This is our band," I informed him. "If you'll recall, the advert stated that our duo is holding auditions for a rhythm section."

"Well, actually, your ad wasn't very clear," the violinist countered. Steve went on to explain that he'd had the impression that we were chick vocalists looking for backup musicians. I sucked in my breath, and slowly exhaled. Had Emily Muff's classified ad not been clear? Still, there was something about this guy named Steve that continued to pique our interest, and we asked him to have a seat.

My bandmate and I gave Steve a run-down on the history of Emily Muff, and he proved to be an avid listener. When we had finished our account, he acknowledged that our duo had certainly had its ups and downs. "Still . . . if you don't mind . . . I'd like to carry on with the audition," he declared. I glanced around the empty vestibule. It was obvious that Emily Muff had not been besieged by a multitude of drummers and bass players lining up at the door. So, I nodded at Janet, and we decided to give this guy named Steve a listen. The two of us waited as he unfastened the clasp on his violin case. Then he took the instrument out, hooked up its electric pickup, and began applying resin to the bow. When Steve tucked the violin under his chin, I wondered whether his appearance in our lives would signal the end of Emily Muff as a duo.

Em and I picked up the twin Telecasters and swung their straps over our shoulders. Then the three of us tuned our instruments together. Next, Janet and I began playing a medley of our duo's original songs. Steve followed along, and the notes of his violin blended in astonishingly well with Emily Muff's music. As we continued to jam on several other numbers, it became clear that he had an uncanny knack for anticipating our duo's rapid tempo changes—and an instinctive understanding of the emotional themes underlying our songs.

When the final notes of our medley faded away, I could no longer deny that, although Steve was not the bassist or drummer we had been searching for, he might be a cool addition to Emily Muff.

"Hey, not bad!" Janet exclaimed as he lowered the bow to his side. I nodded my head, and grinned at him.

"Yeah! Your violin sounded great! It definitely enhanced our songs," I chimed in. Steve told us that he knew we weren't looking for a violinist, but he had grooved on our sound, and would love to join the band. He placed his instrument back in its case, and then stared at the two of us with a look of hopeful expectation. Em glanced in my direction. I could tell that she wanted to speak with me alone, so we told Steve that the two of us needed a couple of minutes to discuss things in private. He picked up his violin and wandered into the adjoining room, where an empty concession stand was located. Once Steve had disappeared from view, my friend and I began conferring together in hushed tones.

"So, what do you think. Is this guy for real?" I asked. Janet shrugged her shoulders and said that, although Steve was clearly a terrific musician who sounded great with our duo, she was still concerned that we hadn't found a rhythm section yet. I jokingly replied that maybe before we offered Steve a spot, we should audition all of the drummers and bass players who were beating down the door at Studio 51. Obviously, it was difficult for us to deal with the piss-poor turn-out we'd had that day, especially since our duo had toured extensively throughout Britain, and had also been approached by Reprise Records.

"Listen Moo! At this moment we need to focus on deciding what we're going to do about this violinist cat, okay?" my bandmate reasoned. I knew that she was right. Even though we hadn't envisioned a violinist in our line-up, Steve's playing had blended remarkably well with our songs.

So, we decided to offer him a spot in our band.

Soon, Emily Muff began rehearsals as a trio at London's Country Club venue. This facility featured an auditorium with a stage that could be hired as a rehearsal space or performance venue. It was also the same theater where Lew had booked our (refurbished) band for its debut gig.

Chapter Forty-Four

Ginger Jam

One afternoon, I arrived early at the Country Club, hoping to squeeze in a mini-practice session of my own before Janet and Steve arrived for Emily Muff's rehearsal. As usual, the club's manager, Stu, greeted me with a friendly smile when I entered the lobby. In addition to the Fender Telecaster guitar and flute that I was carrying, my jacket pockets were bulging with various blues harmonicas.

"Come on in, Kathy! All set for your rehearsal session?"

"Hello, Stu! How's it going?" He told me that his studio was heavily booked, and that business was doing well. I mentioned that I had arrived early for rehearsal, and was hoping to grab a couple of minutes to practice on my own. Stu seemed like he was about to reply, when the telephone rang in his office nearby. He waved to me, and hurried to answer it. Once he had disappeared from view, I headed towards the auditorium.

As I rounded the corner into the theater, I halted in the entranceway. I'd expected that the rehearsal hall would be empty but, instead, there was a guy sitting on a stool in the middle of a massive drum kit that had been set up center stage. The name "Ginger Baker" was stenciled in white on the bass drum. I recognized that this man with the red beard, fly-away hair, and long, narrow face was, indeed, the famous percussionist himself. At that moment, his attention was focused on making adjustments to the hi-hat, and he didn't notice me standing there. Once Ginger Baker seemed satisfied that everything was in order, he picked up a pair of drumsticks and began playing a wildly driving beat.

Although I wondered why Stu hadn't mentioned that Ginger Baker was in the building, I was glad the drummer seemed unaware of my presence. This enabled me to slip unnoticed into one of the seats at the back of the auditorium, which was hidden in the shadows. Knowing that I might be privy to watching him play several rounds before his solo rehearsal ended, I felt fortunate to have arrived early for Emily Muff's rehearsal. As I continued to eavesdrop on Ginger Baker's private session, he began playing another series of complex, driving beats, and I was mesmerized by the waves of raw, earthy energy that he was unleashing throughout the theater.

I knew that he had performed with other esteemed musicians, including Alexis Korner and Graham Bond, as well as Eric Clapton and Jack Bruce in the band Cream. He had also founded his band Ginger Baker's Air Force, and I had seen him play with the supergroup Blind Faith at its debut gig in Hyde Park. Although Ginger Baker had performed for sold-out crowds world-wide, witnessing his solo practice that day at the Country Club was a real eye-opener for me. It was obvious that he had no need to perform in front of an audience in order to play from the depths of his soul—and I finally understood first-hand why he was so revered in the rock music scene.

When I "came to" at the end of his rehearsal session, the drummer was wiping his sweaty face with a worn-out towel. Once he started packing up his belongings, I rose from my seat, grabbed my instruments, and cautiously approached the stage. I knew that it had been presumptuous of me to have eavesdropped on his solo session, yet I wanted him to know how truly honored I had been to have witnessed his extraordinary drumming that day.

As I emerged from the shadows at the back of the theater, Ginger Baker glanced up and stared at me. Before he had a chance to speak, I explained how I had arrived early for my band's rehearsal, and that I hoped he didn't mind my hanging around during his session. He said it was okay, and I told him how his drumming had moved me, heart and soul. "Glad you liked it," he replied. Ginger Baker continued to chat with me, mostly in monosyllables, for another minute or so before he gathered up the remainder of his personal gear, and split the club. After he left, I sat down on the edge of the stage, and gazed at his drum kit.

Ginger Baker's powerful, rhythmic patterns were still reverberating through my mind when Em and Steve arrived at the Country Club several minutes later.

"See any rock stars around here today?" Janet quipped.

How could I begin to explain the extent to which I had been blown away by Ginger Baker's incredible drumming during his solo session? As Em waited for my reply, she suddenly noticed the name stenciled on the bass drum, and her eyebrows arched upwards. "Oh, no! Don't tell me I just missed Ginger Baker . . ." she grumbled. Steve's eyes had opened wide, as well, and I nodded at the two of them.

"Yup! He just finished his rehearsal session a little while ago," I announced. "You should have heard him jamming, guys! His drumming was outta sight!" I went on to explain that I had arrived early at the Country Club, hoping to squeeze in some practice time of my own before Emily Muff's rehearsal began. Instead, I'd stumbled upon Ginger Baker drumming away during his solo practice time. Janet sighed, and said that she couldn't believe my luck.

"It pays to be a compulsive chick rocker!" I replied with a grin.

Chapter Forty-Five

Crashing
the Mega-Session

When Lew learned that we still had not found a drummer or bass player for our band, he expressed his displeasure at the news. However, he continued to provide representation for our group, and had booked Emily Muff into London's Trident Studios to record a demo tape. Lew indicated that he would be present at this session, and we would be playing our own instruments for the demo. He also wanted several of our musician friends from Mighty Baby present at the studio to further embellish our sound. Once the tape was completed, he planned to shop it around at an upcoming music festival that was to be held on the Continent.

Em and I felt right at home while setting up our instruments at Trident Studios on the day of the session, and pleased that Lew was there. In addition to Steve and the recording engineer, Martin and several of his bandmates were on the scene, as well. A part-time percussionist we knew named Jack, who had basic drumming skills, had also arrived. Introductions were made, and it felt gratifying to finally be making a demo tape that featured Emily Muff originals.

After a couple of songs had been recorded, it was clear that the embellished renditions made the music sound fuller. It seemed that one of them, however, "Country Air," had morphed into an almost unrecognizable number that sounded overly slick, and a bit corny, as well. I was perturbed about this, but decided not to force the issue. When the next track was about to be recorded, Em began counting in the song. That take went exceedingly well, as did the recording of the next several numbers. By the middle of Emily Muff's session, we had the makings of an official demo tape, and Lew was grinning from ear-to-ear. Janet and I requested that everyone take a break, and the two of us headed for the Ladies Room to freshen up.

As soon as we stepped into the lobby, my "Rolling Stones Radar" revved into high alert. I looked around, and my eyes zeroed in on drummer Charlie Watts chatting with Mick Jagger. They were standing at the bottom of a staircase that led to an adjacent recording studio. "Looks like we're about to cross paths with the Rolling Stones again!" I chortled. Several seconds later, Janet had spotted them, too.

"Ohhh! It's them, all right!" she exclaimed. "But what'll we do now, Moo? After we rejected Mick and Keith at Olympic, I doubt they'll invite us to hang out with them at their studio *this* time." As she spoke, there seemed to be a hint of sadness in her voice. It made me wonder whether she harbored any secret regrets that Emily Muff had turned down the Glimmer Twins during Mighty Baby's recording session at Olympic.

"I have to confess that I've thought about that night a million times," I muttered. The two of us continued to loiter in the lobby, soaking up the sight of Charlie and Mick chatting together, as they made their way up the stairs into their studio. My friend and I remained motionless, in order to avoid appearing too over-eager. It was obvious that we needed to decide whether we were going to crash their recording session. Even though we were antsy to do so, we also knew that Lew was no doubt wondering where we'd wandered off to. Janet and I continued to grapple with our emotions for all of *ten seconds*, and then I nudged her. "Well, Em . . . it's now or never . . ." I began. She flashed me an impish grin, and we both dashed off in the direction that Mick and Charlie had taken.

After heading up the staircase, we paused for a moment outside the entrance to the studio. There was no one in sight, so we opened the door and stepped inside. Although I half-expected a burly bouncer to be blocking our way (or Mick and Keith glaring at us), there was only one guy standing near the door. He appeared to be paying no attention to Em and me, so the two of us wandered further inside the control room. We glanced around, and noticed that several guys were hanging out near the mixing board. What looked like an assortment of groupies and girlfriends were clustered near the plate-glass window that overlooked the studio below. Janet and I made our way through the crowd, and managed to secure a spot where we could press our noses against the window pane, and ogle the tableau in the studio below. Surrounded by an array of instruments and electrical equipment, Mick Jagger, Keith Richards, Charlie Watts, and a bass player I didn't recognize, were conferring together. Although my nose felt as though it was glued to the glass, I was mesmerized by Mick as he sashayed over to his microphone. Charlie Watts sat down at his kit and began playing a series of jazzy drum rolls. The bassist was re-tuning his instrument, and Keith Richards began rockin' out the studio with a series of flashy bar chords on his Gibson guitar. Soon, they had eased into one of their numbers, and the tape was rolling.

As they played, there seemed to be a laid-back, yet professional vibe in the studio below. I felt honored to be present at this Rolling Stones session, and was sure that my bandmate must have felt the same. At the same time, we also knew that Emily Muff had its *own* recording session to finish. So, we took a final look at the rock stars below, and headed towards the exit. The same bouncer who had been standing inside the door when we first arrived was still at his post. He glanced at the two of us, and smiled.

"Emily Muff! How's it going, girls?" he wanted to know. Janet told him that we were doing great.

"You recognized us . . ." I blurted out. The young man nodded.

"Course I did, Luv!" he replied. "Otherwise I wouldn't 'ave let you in, now . . . would I?" He went on to tell us that he'd been to several Emily Muff gigs, as well. Suddenly, Janet began to chuckle, and said that we were wondering whether drummer Charlie Watts would like to join our band.

"Dream on," I muttered, and the three of us laughed together.

It had been an amazing opportunity to attend a Rolling Stones recording session at Trident Studios, and it was also cool that Emily Muff had been recognized by a member of their entourage. I was still floating on a natural high when my bandmate and I retraced our steps down the stairs. As we entered the control room of Emily Muff's recording session, Lew glared at the two of us. Janet and I apologized for our tardiness. However, we remained mum about our foray into Mick and Keith's domain and, luckily, Lew didn't question us.

Buoyed up by having witnessed the Rolling Stones rockin' out in the studio nearby, Janet and I picked up our instruments, and we were instantly back in the groove. The next several hours of Emily Muff's session was smooth-sailing, and a demo tape was well on its way to completion. Although the majority of tracks had been finished by then, there were still a few more songs to record. Fortunately, Lew had booked some extra blocks of time at Trident for the next day in which to wrap up these numbers.

Emily Muff's follow-up recording session went smoothly. By the end of the allotted time, we had a professional demo tape, and Lew was beaming with pride. While the equipment was being packed up, Janet and I told him how much we appreciated the opportunity to record a demo of Emily Muff originals, and he continued to confer with us for several minutes. We also hung out with our bandmate Steve for a while. Then she and I thanked everyone else for helping us out, and the recording session was officially over.

On our way home, we chatted about how exciting it was to have (finally!) been able to make a demo tape of our songs. Unlike Tony at Olympic, Lew had understood the importance of allowing us to record Emily Muff originals—and to play our own instruments on the tracks, as well. Later that evening, the two of us were still feeling euphoric. "Man! What a week!" Janet exclaimed. "We just finished recording our demo tape, and also got to hang out at a Rolling Stones recording session!" I nodded, and reminded her that it was also cool that we had been recognized by the guy from Mick and Keith's crew. Janet playfully wagged a finger at me.

"Now, remember, Moo! We can't let it go to our heads!" she chortled.

"Too late! It already has!"

Em and I grinned at each other—and then we burst out laughing.

Chapter Forty-Six

Bass and Drum Quandary

Soon after the recording of Emily Muff's demo tape, our trio finally expanded into a four-piece band when friends of ours introduced us to a bassist named Nick. Although our buddy Jack continued to fill in periodically, he was not a professional drummer, so Janet and I continued to be on the lookout for a more experienced percussionist.

Nick was a competent bass player, and rehearsals seemed to be going well. During one of our practice sessions, however, he dropped the bombshell that he was moving out of London to shack up with his girlfriend. "What a drag! I can't believe Nick dumped our band for some chick," I exclaimed at our next rehearsal session. Everyone agreed that his departure had definitely left Emily Muff in the lurch. So, we began searching for a new bass player.

In the meantime, Lew informed us of the exciting news that Liberty/UA had offered to sign Emily Muff to its record label—and we were ecstatic at the news! Yet I privately remained concerned how Lew would react when he found out that we had not yet secured a rhythm section for our band. Around this same time period, I moved in with Janet. The flat was located in West Hampstead, and featured two bedrooms, a tiny kitchen, and shared bathroom. After finding out that a rehearsal studio had opened up in the neighborhood, we stopped by to check it out. It was operated by an organist named Rod, who was the brother of bluesman John Mayall. We soon booked Emily Muff into this facility for some much-needed practice time before Lew was to return to London. After listening to Emily Muff rehearse at his studio several times, Rod asked to sit in with us on his Hammond organ for an informal jam session. "I have a hunch that he's interested in joining our band," Janet remarked as we headed home from one of our rehearsal sessions.

"Yeah, I've had the same impression, Em. Still, no matter how skilled Rod is as an organist, we need to remember that we're not looking for another keyboardist." As I spoke, the two of us turned left onto Pandora Road. I glanced up at the street sign, and found myself wondering whether we would be opening a Pandora's Box if we were to offer Rod a spot in our band. Despite our initial misgivings about adding an organist to Emily Muff's line-up, Lew's insistence that we have a rhythm section in place reminded me of the intimidation we had encountered at Reprise. Em and I had tried . . . and tried . . . to find both a bassist and drummer for our group. With the exception of Nick, who had soon split the scene, we had not yet secured a replacement (male or female) for him—nor the drummer that our manager was demanding we add by the time of our "debut" gig at the Country Club.

"If Lew wants Emily Muff to have a rhythm section so badly, why hasn't he come up with a drummer and bassist for our duo *himself?*" I pointed out. Janet nodded and reminded us that the concept of two chicks playing electric guitars was still not widely accepted in Britain. This had, no doubt, made it even harder for us to find a rhythm section for our band. I thought about Emily Muff's touring days with the Leicester Lads. "I don't think Family expected us to add a male rhythm section when they named our duo Emily Muff," I wisecracked as we unlocked the front door of the house. The two of us made our way up the staircase and then entered our flat. Once we sat down in the kitchen, the conversation switched to our demo session at Trident studios.

During this discussion, we recalled that, although the music had seemed fuller, one of our songs had sounded very different, almost corny at times. "And that's one of the reasons why I'm still partial to Emily Muff as a duo," I reiterated. Janet said she agreed with me, and the two of us were silent for several minutes. We then began conversing about Lew and the status of our band. It was obvious that he had been covering both our living and rehearsal expenses. Because of this, both Janet and I were starting to feel pressured into asking Rod to join our band.

"What's so friggin' ironic is that we know that Emily Muff doesn't need another keyboard player," my friend groaned.

"Tell me about it, Em! We both play keyboards, so it's not like we'd be adding anything new . . ."

Rod was certainly not the rhythm section that our manager was insisting we add to our lineup. Yet time was running out for Emily

Muff to meet Lew's demands. Janet and I sat up late into the night, discussing the pros and cons of inviting Rod to join our band. Finally, after going back and forth for what seemed like ages, we decided to make him an offer because he helped to create a fuller sound. When we told Rod the news the following day, he agreed to join our band. We also asked our buddy Jack to back us up on drums again and, soon, we were rehearsing at Rod's studio as a five-piece band.

At first, our practice sessions seemed to be working out well. It was not long, however, before more and more time began being wasted on what seemed to be petty issues—and I began to feel that familiar sinking feeling in the pit of my stomach. When Em and I returned home after one especially awkward rehearsal, we reminisced about how there had never been bickering like this in our two-person format. Most of all, it was clear that the music was no longer flowing smoothly. By then, it was obviously too late to make any further changes. Lew was on his way back to London and, at that point, we had no choice but to present our five-piece group at the Country Club as scheduled.

On the night of the show, the audience seemed to groove on our set, yet Em and I knew better. We were well-aware that the two of us had succumbed to mounting pressure from Lew to augment our sound. Our supposedly refurbished band had never really gotten off the ground in the first place—and the overall performance at the Country Club that night seemed lackluster, at best.

Chapter Forty-Seven

A Metallic Hue

After the show that night, Lew was a man of few words. Instead of offering us feedback about the band's performance, he requested that members of Emily Muff meet with him the following day at the hotel where he was staying. When Janet, Steve, and I arrived at Lew's lodgings at the appointed time, he greeted us in the lobby with a stony expression on his face. He then led the three of us to a spacious, circular table and motioned for everyone to have a seat. Several minutes later, Rod and Jack entered the hotel. I waved to them, and they joined us at the table.

Once everyone had been seated, Lew spread out several, official-looking documents before him. He then proceeded to tell us that Emily Muff's performance at the Country Club had not come close to matching the terrific sound that had been achieved on its demo tape. He scowled at Janet and me, and reminded us that he had asked Emily Muff to have a rhythm section securely in place by the time he returned to London. According to Lew, our band had Steve who was talented violinist, Jack who was not a professional drummer, and Rod on keyboards.

The businessman leaned forward in his seat. "What were you thinking?" he bellowed. We watched as Lew scooped up one of the documents that was lying on the table in front of him. Then he ripped it in two, and crumpled it in his fist with a dramatic flair. As I stared at the mangled wad of paper in his hand, my mind was inwardly shrieking, "Oh! No! *Not again!*"

I opened my mouth to speak, but Janet had opened hers, and was already defending Emily Muff. Lew paid no attention to what she was saying. Instead, he announced that he was no longer prepared to make the five of us an official deal.

"What? You're not offering us a contract?" one of my other new bandmates exclaimed.

"Well, that's what it looks like, doesn't it" Lew retorted.

No one said another word—until I finally spoke up.

"Now hold on a minute, Lew!" I began. "Janet and I were just trying to enhance our sound, like you asked us to do. We did find one bass player, but he quit the band almost immediately because he was moving away from London to be with his girlfriend. Our band's been searching for a new bassist ever since, and we're still looking for a drummer. Janet and I have tried *everything* in our power to make it happen. But it seems like you keep blaming us. Frankly, I haven't seen you making any effort to find us a rhythm section."

As I spoke, Lew continued to glare at everyone. He then motioned for Rod and Jack to depart, and requested that the remaining members of Emily Muff stay seated at the table. An awkward silence ensued, and I watched as Jack and Rod slowly rose from their chairs. I felt mortified . . . as though Janet and I had been personally responsible for letting them down. To me, no matter what Lew had yet to offer, it would be a bittersweet victory for the remaining members of Emily Muff.

Once Jack and Rod had exited the building, Lew slid a second document across the table towards Janet, Steve and me. He then proceeded to outline several marketing strategies he had devised to promote Emily Muff as a trio. As he spoke, it seemed as though he was expecting females in the band to wear form-fitting dresses made of an eye-catching, metallic hue at Emily Muff's performances. The rousing lyrics of the Janis Ian song, "Society's Child" echoed through my mind as I listened to his latest demands.

"This is one of your marketing strategies?" Em was asking.

"Yeah, I can't believe you're saying this, Lew!' I countered. "You're the one who said you'd have our best interests at heart, remember? We thought that you understood we want audiences to focus on our music." Janet leaned across the table towards the businessman.

"Emily Muff plays rock, you dig?" she insisted. "It's not a female vocal group that wears glittery, slinky dresses." Lew shook his head and scowled. Up until that point, I had mistakenly assumed that he was a manager/producer who would be hip to our band's philosophical stance. Instead, his true colors had finally emerged, and they had a distinctly metallic hue. Given my new understanding of things, I was no longer sure that I wished to be associated with Lew—even though it might mean that Emily Muff would lose the opportunity to sign with the Liberty/UA label.

I reached across the conference table and slid the (intact) document back towards him. "If you insist on having this kind of attitude regarding what's left of our band . . . then you can keep your contract," I fumed. Janet nodded her head and rose from the table. Steve and I got up from our chairs, as well. As the three of us made our way towards the main entrance, we could hear Lew yelling something to the effect that Emily Muff would be hearing from his attorney.

It was clear that yet another layer of Em and Moo's näiveté had peeled away during that fateful meeting. "Never again will I allow a music mogul to try and manipulate our image," I silently vowed.

I held my head up high as the three of us walked out of the hotel lobby.

Chapter Forty-Eight

Doing Our Thing

Emily Muff was finally free from yet another music mogul's attempt to manipulate its image. Yet there were moments when Janet and I wondered whether we'd *ever* find a manager eager to promote our original songs—while not demanding that we make drastic changes to our wardrobe, or lineup. It was a well-known fact that many rock groups relied upon their sexy image in order to bolster sales. I had to admit that watching a male musician strut around onstage in his skintight trousers definitely had its moments. However, Em and I were trailblazers, paving the way for female rockers in the future. We didn't want these women to experience the same sexist attitudes and boorish behaviors that we had encountered. The two of us were trend-setters of a different breed. Instead of wearing low-cut, slinky outfits, we preferred that audiences concentrate on the tightness of our music.

When Family's manager, Tony Gourvish, heard the news that Emily

Muff had split with Lew, he offered to provide representation again for our band. We were pleased to hear from him, especially since he had never pressured us to add a rhythm section. In fact, Em and I had privately held out hope that we would, one day, be able to patch up our differences with Lotus, and move forward with a lucrative record deal. His reappearance in our lives could not have come at a more opportune time. I was so excited at the prospect of returning to the Family fold that I dashed out a quick letter to my parents in New York:

Dear Mom and Dad,

Tony Gourvish contacted us recently and expressed an interest in managing our band again. Now that Emily Muff's back with Bradgate Bush, Family's lawyer has agreed to meet with us and take on our case against Lew. It sure is nice for our rock group to finally have management on our side!

Love, Kathy.

In the meantime, Lew did not hesitate to go after Emily Muff with a vengeance. Luckily, our attorney stepped up in defense of us over what the American businessman claimed was Emily Muff's breach of contract. Finally, it was agreed to let our band out of its so-called contract, with the stipulation that all of the equipment Lew had purchased for us would be confiscated by his company. In addition, he was apparently demanding a profit from the sale of Emily Muff's first, second, and third record albums. Although Bradgate Bush was outraged by this, Tony was advised to accept the deal, in order to prevent Lew from securing additional revenue from the sale of Emily Muff's subsequent albums.

Once the legal hassle with Lew had finally been resolved, Lotus informed us that producer Trevor Lucas of Island Records was interested in auditioning Emily Muff. Janet and I had previously heard about Trevor's innovative style, and we were eager for our trio to make his acquaintance. When the day of our appointment to meet with Tony and Trevor arrived, Em and I were especially pleased to see that Lotus had made sure to be present for the occasion. After giving them a run-down on the status of our group, Janet, Steve, and I played a selection of Emily Muff's originals, including "First Song" and "The Bird It Flew."

Our trio played well and, after the audition, Trevor expressed an interest in working with our band. He suggested that we record a new demo tape, and also proposed that we add a rhythm section in order to augment our sound. Although I had initially been pleased to hear that this well-respected record producer was interested in Emily Muff, his request that we add a rhythm section set off a series of alarm bells in my head.

Hadn't we been down this road before?

Janet must have been thinking along the same lines; she began describing the various roadblocks Emily Muff had encountered in its search for a rhythm section. Upon hearing our story, Trevor acknowledged that it might be tough to find a competent rhythm section. However, he continued to urge our trio to re-open the search, and said that he would be back in touch with Tony soon.

The Island Records producer rose from his seat and shook our hands. Lotus stood up, as well, and nodded at Emily Muff before he and Trevor left the room.

After Janet and I arrived home later, we began chatting about Emily Muff's audition that afternoon. It wasn't long before the two of us were discussing Trevor, and how he wanted us to add a rhythm section to our band. "Cripes! I almost fell out of my chair when that topic was raised," I exclaimed.

"Me, too!" Janet replied. She went on to say that, since Tony had never pressured us to add a rhythm section, she had assumed that Trevor would feel the same. I shook my head and groaned.

"Here we go again making a bunch of friggin' assumptions. Maybe we should have asked Lotus to hang around after the meeting, so we could have spoken with him privately."

"Neither of these guys has a clue how hard we've tried to find a rhythm section . . ."

"Or how much we love Emily Muff as a duo!" I mused.

During the silence that followed, I thought about all the shows that our duo had opened for the band Family. Em and I had *always* been in sync as Britain's First Female Rock Duo—and our performances reflected this special connection. When it came to writing our songs, it seemed like the two of us had breathed life into them as one.

Deep in my heart . . . I did not want it any other way.

And neither did Janet.

Within days, Em and I had accepted a gig at London's Roundhouse venue, where DJ Jeff Dexter had invited Emily Muff to open the show as a duo for the band America. While this male trio was primarily a folk/rock act, Emily Muff continued to showcase songs featuring Rickenbacker and Fender Telecaster electric guitars, keyboards, blues harmonicas, and flute. When the day of the Roundhouse gig rolled around, it seemed as though members of America were surprised that two Telecaster-toting females had been booked on the same bill as their folk/rock group.

Our performance at the Roundhouse marked a turning point in Emily Muff's career. We had a *blast* performing as a duo once again. Deep in our hearts, Janet and I knew that we had wasted enough time listening to what other people had envisioned for us. As trailblazing rocker chicks, it was time for Em and Moo to be true to ourselves and follow the T. Rex adage, "Get It On!"

Once we made the decision to reinstate our band as a duo, Janet and I broke the news to Tony. Needless to say, Lotus was far from pleased about our decision, and our relationship with him quickly began to unravel again. Despite the fact that we had blown the opportunity to work with both Lotus and Trevor, my bandmate and I were adamant about our decision. All that remained for us to do was break the news to Steve.

Although I had stoically volunteered to carry out this most difficult task, I was unprepared for my emotional meeting with the violinist at his flat. "Can't say I'm surprised," he replied upon hearing the news.

"Aggh! I feel so awful, Steve! You're a terrific musician, and none of this is your fault. Janet and I just think it's best that we go back to being a duo." The violinist gave my arm an affectionate squeeze and told me that, even though he was disappointed to no longer be a member of the group, he had always felt that Janet and I had a special sound—as a duo.

I was grateful that Steve understood why Em and I had decided to return to our two-person format, and pleased that my friendship with him continued to thrive even after he had left the band.

Chapter Forty-Nine

Quintessence

Around the same time that Emily Muff officially regrouped as a duo, Janet befriended members of a London-based rock band called Quintessence. Not long afterwards, they invited us to tour Britain with them as their support group. Em and I were honored to have this opportunity, and excited to learn that Quintessence was scheduled to wrap up its UK tour that year with a Christmas Concert on the 20th of December 1971 at London's Royal Albert Hall.

Janet and I had always envisioned performing at this illustrious venue, and now this dream was about to come true! We began writing new songs and, soon, our duo was touring throughout Great Britain with Quintessence. It was exciting to be back on the road, opening shows at many of the concert halls where we had previously been booked with Family and other well-known rock groups.

Quintessence was known as a psychedelic, progressive rock band.

Also reflected in its music were both jazz and Eastern Indian influences. Many of their fans were hip to the spiritual themes of peace, love, and meditation. It was obvious that the music of Quintessence was more mellow than the majority of rock bands Emily Muff opened shows for on the circuit. In fact, there were times when I secretly missed the nightly excitement of Family's powerhouse performances. On the other hand, it was quite refreshing that female fans in the audience at Quintessence gigs seemed less inclined to apply make-up during the opening act.

Janet and I were having a wonderful time touring and, suddenly, the Quintessence Christmas concert was fast approaching. Numerous publicity posters announcing the upcoming event were being plastered up in Tube stations, on billboards, kiosks, fences, walkways, and roundabouts throughout London. "It's so cool seeing all of these posters for the Albert Hall Christmas concert, isn't it, Moo?" my bandmate exclaimed during one of our rehearsal sessions.

"It sure is! If they weren't glued so well to the surfaces they're pasted on, I'd be tempted to rip one of them off as a souvenir," I confessed with a chuckle.

It was a heady feeling for our chick rock duo to be opening the concert at this world-renown venue, and I continued to express my excitement. "Ohh! Think of it Em! Soon we'll be playing on the same stage where the Stones, Cream, the Who, Led Zeppelin, Pink Floyd, and Bob Dylan have performed!" Janet grinned.

"We've wanted our duo to play the Albert Hall ever since we saw the Incredible String Band's concert there back in '68," she mused.

"Yeah, those days seem so long ago, don't they, Em? You and I were a couple of naïve chick rockers back then, weren't we?"

"That's for sure!"

We smiled to ourselves, each reflecting upon how fortunate our duo had been to go straight on tour, opening shows at concert halls for big-name acts. "Seriously, Moo," Janet remarked. "I hope female musicians in the future won't forget that it was courageous chick rockers like Emily Muff who struggled back in the sixties, and helped pave the way for their bands." I nodded my head, and said that I felt we had become stronger women for having grappled with the many obstacles we had encountered.

"If Emily Muff had sold out for Reprise, or opted to wear slinky dresses like Lew was demanding, who knows how different our duo might have been forced to become? At least you and I have the satisfaction of knowing that we never compromised ourselves with regard to our music—or our principles, for that matter."

As Janet and I continued to reflect upon our journey, we looked back with gratitude and pride at our many accomplishments. After all, we had:

Co-founded the trailblazing chick rock duo Emily Muff.

Toured the rock music circuit throughout Great Britain.

Been approached by Reprise, Liberty/UA,
and Island Records.

Appeared on both BBC Wales-TV and BBC London-TV.

Chapter Fifty

Triumph at the Royal Albert Hall

On the afternoon of the Quintessence Christmas Concert, there were ice crystals on the ground, but the sun had been peeking out all day—and my mood was buoyant. When Em and I arrived at the Royal Albert Hall, we were issued a pair of Performer passes at the artists' entrance. Next, our rock duo was escorted to its spacious dressing room by a staff member of the venue. As the two of us entered the changing area, we glanced around at its elaborate décor.

"We've sure come a long way since we had to rig up that make-shift dressing room at the Marquee Club, eh?" I observed.

"Speaking of reminiscing, I've been thinking about Lots Road and the day that Tony Kaye 'discovered' our duo."

"Yeah, and I'll never forget his words of encouragement, too!" I replied.

The two of us began unpacking our white floor-length dresses. Quintessence had requested that all performers wear white for this special Christmas concert. So, Em and I changed into our white outfits later for the upcoming dress rehearsal. As we were primping in the mirror, a member of the crew told us that our soundcheck was coming up in a couple of minutes. When we arrived in the wings, I noticed that a large portion of the stage was filled with colorful, fresh flowers. Their beauty and fragrance were breathtaking, and so was the vastness of the Royal Albert Hall. I felt the thrill of anticipation as Em and I gazed at the rows upon rows of seats arranged in tiers throughout the rotund arena. Later, the ticket holders queued up outside the theater would be taking their seats, and waiting for the show to begin

Although Emily Muff had performed in front of capacity crowds at numerous concert halls throughout Great Britain, London's Royal Albert Hall had over 5,200 seats. This was the largest venue we had played on our various tours, and I felt a fresh wave of tingly anticipation.

"Well, Moo, we're finally playing *the big one*," Em whispered in my ear as the two of us made our way towards center stage for our soundcheck. We grabbed our Rickenbacker and Telecaster guitars, and stepped up to the microphones. As I swung my guitar strap over my shoulder and glanced out into the colossal arena, the Neil Young song title, "Expecting to Fly" came to mind. This was one of the happiest days of my life, and my heart was soaring!

My flute and Hohner harmonicas had already been lined up on top of a nearby amplifier, so we checked the tuning of our guitars. I grinned at Em, and she smiled back at me. In the meantime, the sound man at the PA station was requesting that we do a quick medley of our songs. So, the two of us began to play.

"Feeling the answer,
Feeling the answer.
Silver curtain partly open.
I see that white is his cloak
Of serenity.
All that I see leads into immortality,
All that I see leads into immortality . . ."

After running through several other original numbers, we were pleased that our soundcheck had gone without a hitch. My friend and I headed towards the wings, where the lead singer of Quintessence, "Shiva," was waiting. He was clothed in a flowing white robe that made him look like a life-sized Adonis. As we chatted with him on the sidelines, other members of Quintessence joined us there. We conversed about the upcoming concert, and the beauty of the flowers surrounding us, until they headed onstage for their soundcheck.

After the dress-rehearsal was officially over, Em and I hung out with our friends for a while, and then the two of us headed backstage. We were just making the final touches to our hair, when a group of smiling fans and well-wishers began streaming backstage. Soon, the doors to the concert hall had been opened to ticketholders, and the seats were filling up all the way to the highest rows of seats.

Before we knew it, the sold-out venue was filled to capacity, and Janet and I were standing in the wings, poised to make our entrance.

In less than a minute, the two of us were dashing onstage. Waves of applause greeted us as we reached for our Rickenbacker and Telecaster guitars, and checked their tuning. Next, my bandmate stepped up to her microphone and greeted the thousands of patrons in the audience with a dazzling smile.

"This instrumental, called 'Essence' is for you," she announced.

As soon as the two of us began to play, the notes soared upwards towards the topmost tier—and I smiled to myself. The audience seemed swept up by the music, as well, and gave our duo an enthusiastic round of applause. Our next number featured bluesy Hohner harmonica, piano, and two-part harmonies. Janet also sang lead, her voice powerful and compelling.

"Love is the force

That gathers us . . .

Drink the wine of Truth with him.

For he has chosen you,

Again.

Brothers are we,

On the road,

On the road . . ."

Em and I were totally in sync with each other, and I felt a rush of euphoria envelop me. All that we had worked so hard to achieve had led up to this . . .

Our rock duo's glorious performance at London's Royal Albert Hall!

As our music echoed throughout the venue, scores of flashbulbs popped high and low, like firefly sparks of light illuminating the concert hall. In between numbers, we smiled at one another, confident in the knowledge that we were playing our best gig ever. Soon, I was making my way over to the piano, while my bandmate re-tuned her guitar. Our music was melodic, and the flowers around us fragrant as our harmonies soared throughout London's Royal Albert Hall.

When the notes of our final number faded away, Em and I savored the resounding applause for Britain's First Female Rock Duo.

We grinned at each other . . .

Bowed to the sold-out crowd . . .

And then we raised our arms up high in the air.

Epilogue

After the Quintessence Christmas concert at London's Royal Albert Hall, Em and Moo's female rock duo was booked for an upcoming tour with them the following spring. During the intervening period, Janet and Kathy went on holiday to New York, and Em became engaged to an actor she had met there. They soon married, and Emily Muff disbanded.

After a sojourn in Woodstock, New York, Janet and her husband relocated to Los Angeles. She resumed writing music, entered the corporate world, advanced to a prominent position, and also remarried.

Kathy remained in New York, where she kept writing music. She also earned her BA and MSW degrees, and worked as a therapist/ social worker. During her 17-year marriage to a guy she met at a Stones concert, they had a son. She eventually remarried, but it was short-lived. Kathy continues to enjoy writing music, and a review of her song "Inside Out" appeared in *Spectator Magazine*. Several of her original instrumentals have aired worldwide on MUZAK, as well, and she is a member of ASCAP.

The legacy of Emily Muff lives on. As a musician and author, Kathy continues to be interviewed about her experiences as a trailblazing female rocker. She is frequently asked about her advice for young musicians today—and for all those with a vision in their heart:

Don't let anything stop you!

Reach for the stars!

Live your dreams!

Gallery

Emily Muff in Concert.

(Photo by Peter Sanders.)

Having Fun on the Playground!

Budding Keyboardist.

Alan & me with our Beatles albums.

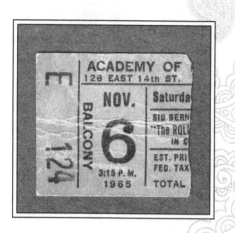

Rolling Stones – My '65 Ticket Stubs

My Upper Deck photo – The Beatles @ Shea Stadium

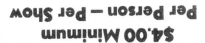

$4.00 Minimum
Per Person — Per Show

**$4.00 Minimum
Per Person — Per Show**

Phone Booth Table Tent Card

Rolling Stones - Autographs

In my cape on Carnaby Street.

STUDIO 51

10-11 Great Newport Street, Leicester Square, W.C.2

MEMBER   NO. 726

Name......................

Address......................

Expires ...JUN 1969......JUN 1969

This Card to be produced at all Club Sessions.

My Membership card to this terrific jazz/blues club.

Hanging out with Derek (my friend/harmonica mentor).

Me (with hat) and Janet at JFK Airport—moving to Britain.

Groovin' on the London life!

Emily Muff's London debut at The Marquee Club.

On tour!

**LEEDS POLYTECHNIC UNION
INAUGURAL BALL**

NICE · FAMILY

with EMILY MUFF

CHICKEN SHACK

TINKERS

Light Shows - Discotheque

FRIDAY, JANUARY 30th

Tickets £1 single, 35/ double,
from Leeds Poly Union, 30171
S U Cards · Dress · Ties

Emily Muff is billed on the same show as The Nice.

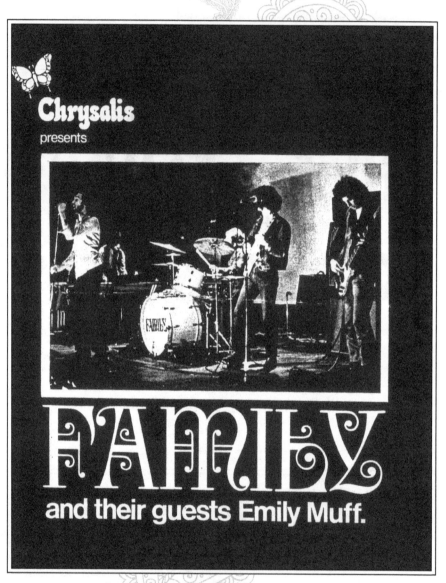

Chrysalis presents

FAMILY

and their guests Emily Muff.

Chrysalis flier for a Family/Emily Muff concert.

Emily Muff demo/copy of Family's "My Way"

—recorded @ Olympic Sound Studios

Chrysalis presents (in association with Bradgate Bush Ltd.)

FAMILY

in concert with their friends

EMILY MUFF

1st MAY—LYCEUM, STRAND	26th MAY—NEWCASTLE
20th MAY—BIRMINGHAM	27th MAY—LIVERPOOL
21st MAY—SHEFFIELD	28th MAY—LEICESTER
24th MAY—BRISTOL MECCA	1st JUNE—GUILDFORD

Touring Great Britain, opening concerts for the band Family.

Exterior view of London's Royal Albert Hall.

(Photo: K. Bushnell, 2014)

QUINTESSENCE
CHRISTMAS CONCERT
Royal Albert Hall
MONDAY 20 DECEMBER 7.30pm

Order your tickets by mail NOW at a special saving by letter, or by sending coupon below

20 Dec. 1971 7.30 p.m.

Performer

ROYAL ALBERT HALL
General Manager: FRANK J. MUNDY

Monday 20 December 1971
at 7.30 p.m.   Doors open 7
QUINTESSENCE
CHRISTMAS CONCERT

PERFORMER
This ticket does not entitle the holder to a seat in the auditorium

NO RE-ADMISSION

Enter by Door No. 1

TO BE RETAINED

Ad for the Quintessence Christmas concert that featured our female rock duo.

Kathy's reunion with Jon Anderson of Yes, @ The Harvester Aug. 13, 2019

About the Author

KATHY BUSHNELL, MSW, is a musician/songwriter and member of ASCAP. Her early ballet lessons at Joffreys, classical piano studies, and performances with a modern dance troupe gave her a creative spirit—and reverence for the arts. By the time she enrolled at New York City's School of Performing Arts, Kathy had been writing songs for several years. She was also an Anglophile and die-hard rock 'n' roll aficionado. To top things off, her maternal grandmother had been a Suffragette. So, it wasn't surprising that, at the age of nineteen, Kathy was living in London and had co-founded Emily Muff, the First Female Rock Duo in Britain.